# False Questions
## Jesus and Our Spiritual Path

### Clement T. DeWall

PUBLISHED BY FIDELI PUBLISHING INC.

© Copyright 2014, Clement T. DeWall

All Rights Reserved.

No part of this book may be reproduced, stored in a retrieval system, or transmitted by any means, electronic, mechanical, photocopying, recording, or otherwise, without written permission from the author.

ISBN: 978-1-60414-831-2

*To my wife, Eileen Mackin
who helped make this book possible*

# Contents

*Introduction* .................................................................................. ix

### CHAPTER 1
**Historical and Cultural Context** ........................................................ 1
    The Physical World ................................................................ 1
    God ............................................................................................ 2
    Human Nature ........................................................................ 3
    Children of Abraham ............................................................ 4
    The Son of Man and the Apocalyptic World View ........ 5
    The Forced Conversion of Galilee ..................................... 7
    The Jewish View of Pagans and Proselytes ..................... 8

### CHAPTER 2
**A Divided Christianity** ................................................................... 10
  **A. Christian Belief** ..................................................................... 12
    The Apocalyptic Message of John the Baptist ............. 12
    Jesus' Apocalyptic Message ............................................. 13
    Paul's Apocalyptic Message ............................................. 14
    Other Apocalyptic Writers ............................................... 15
    How the Apocalyptic Outlook Changed ...................... 15
    Jesus Seen as the Son of Man .......................................... 16
    Interpretations of Jesus and His Crucifixion .............. 18
    Our Answer ........................................................................... 19

### B. Christian Authority .................................................................................. 20
- The Authority Given to the Apostles ............................................ 21
- Peter's Primacy ................................................................................. 23
- Leadership of the Twelve After the Resurrection ....................... 26
- First Letter of Clement .................................................................... 27
- No Overseers in Paul's Churches ................................................... 27
- The Pastoral Epistles ....................................................................... 28
- The Didache ...................................................................................... 29
- Ignatius of Antioch .......................................................................... 30
- Our Answer ....................................................................................... 30

### CHAPTER 3
## Jesus as the Messiah .................................................................................. 31

### A. Jesus as the Son of David .................................................................... 32
- Contradictions with History .......................................................... 32
- Incompatibility of Matthew and Luke .......................................... 33
- Why the Evangelists Could Have Created Their Stories ........... 33
- The Genealogies ............................................................................... 34
- Matthew's Prophecies ..................................................................... 36
- Luke's Leitmotif ................................................................................ 36
- Summary ........................................................................................... 38

### B. Jesus as the Suffering Servant ............................................................ 39
- Mark's Use of Psalm 22 as an Outline for the Passion ............... 39
- The Contrast between the Passion in Mark and Luke ............... 39
- The Suffering Servant of Isaiah ...................................................... 40
- Our Answer ....................................................................................... 41

### CHAPTER 4
## The Passion .................................................................................................. 42

### A. The Plot to Kill Jesus ........................................................................... 43
- The Cleansing of the Temple ......................................................... 43
- John's Version of the Cleansing ..................................................... 45
- Differences Among the Synoptic Gospels ................................... 46
- Proposed Reasons for the Decision to Kill Jesus ........................ 47
- The Temple Complex ...................................................................... 48

Reasons for Jesus' Actions ..................................................49
Jesus and the Merchants .....................................................50
Jesus and the Money Changers .........................................51
The Temple Tax ......................................................................51
Follow the Money ..................................................................52
The High Priesthood .............................................................54
Our Answer .............................................................................55

**B. The Death Sentence** ...................................................................**56**
The Theory of Peasant Rebels ............................................56
The Charge of Insurrection .................................................57
The Theories of Secret Teaching and No Burial ............58
The Charge of Being King of the Jews .............................59
Pilate: "Are you a king?" .......................................................61
Our Answer .............................................................................62
The Sign Above the Cross ...................................................63
The Release of Jesus' Body .................................................63
Release of the Body ..............................................................65
The Burial ................................................................................65

## CHAPTER 5
# Sin and Salvation ............................................................................67

**A. Baptism and Forgiveness** ........................................................**69**
Jewish Proselyte Baptism ....................................................69
The Baptism of John the Baptist ........................................70
Christian Baptism ..................................................................73
Christian Baptism: Jesus' Teaching ...................................75
Christian Baptism: Apostolic Teaching and Practice ...77
Our Answer .............................................................................78

**B. Belief and Forgiveness** ............................................................**79**
The Creed ................................................................................79
The Parable of the Unjust Servant .....................................80
The Woman with the Alabaster Jar ...................................81
The Lord's Prayer ...................................................................83
Our Answer .............................................................................83

**C. Forgiveness in Christian Churches** ...................................................85
   Public Penance.........................................................................85
   Indirect Forgiveness by Remission of Punishment...................86
   Early Church Practice ............................................................87
   Our Answer.............................................................................87

### CHAPTER 6
**Spiritual Adoption** .................................................................89
   The Audience and Teaching of Jesus .....................................90
   What Happens at Conversion.................................................92
   Our Answer.............................................................................94

### CHAPTER 7
**End Times**................................................................................95
   John of Patmos.......................................................................95
   The Letters to the Seven Churches.........................................96
   Plagues and Punishment.........................................................97
   Evil Is Overcome ....................................................................99
   Our Answer........................................................................... 104
   Lessons from the Book of Revelation ................................... 104

### CHAPTER 8
**Our Spiritual Path**................................................................106

**A. Seeing** ................................................................................ 107

**B. Forgiving** ........................................................................... 108

**C. Blessing** ............................................................................. 110

**D. Giving Thanks**....................................................................113

### APPENDIX A
**Mistranslated Words** ............................................................115

### APPENDIX B
**How to Interpret the Bible** ......................................................... **119**
    Problems in the Bible.................................................................. 120
    Interpreting the Gospels.............................................................. 121

### APPENDIX C
**Matthew's Use of Isaiah 7:14** ....................................................**125**

**Suggested References** ................................................................**130**
    Books ............................................................................................ 130
    DVDs ............................................................................................ 132

**Index**..............................................................................................**133**

# Introduction

In the 1960s I taught a religion class to juniors at Mt. Carmel High School in Denver, Colorado. The course for one semester was a summary of Catholic Church history. In the section describing the split between the Catholic Church and the Orthodox, I found a statement reading something like this: "On July 16, 1054, Pope Leo IX excommunicated Michael Cerularius, the patriarch of Constantinople." This meant nothing to my students without more background material. Since history was barely discussed in my theological studies, I had to do some research.

I found ample material in a three-volume work, *A History of the Church*, by Philip Hughes. I discovered that Pope Leo IX had died on April 19, 1054, and there was no pope at the time Cerularius was excommunicated. The textbook was worse than slanted; it was false.

History can have more than one version, and the version taught is the one the winners write. For the story of the schism, two versions of history emerged, the Catholic and the Orthodox.

The two versions became apparent when I read another edition of Philip Hughes's work. The earlier one presented only the Catholic side, with the Greeks and Cerularius in the wrong. Hughes corrected this slanted picture in his later edition, showing how the Catholic cardinals accused Cerularius of bogus crimes and errors, and had no authority to excommunicate.

## False Questions

My beliefs changed as I got deeper into history. Since my teaching days I have reversed many of my theological positions. In the last fifty years theology and biblical studies have made significant strides because of discoveries such as the Dead Sea Scrolls, archeological research and studies of ancient manuscripts and languages.

Significant advances in theology are not surprising, but it is surprising that many theologians, religion teachers, ministers and priests have *not* changed. Just why, I don't know. Maybe educational institutions have lagged behind. Or maybe the clergy have been taught the latest research while failing to pass it on. Perhaps the clergy think the laity cannot handle new insights. Whatever the reasons, there is a discomforting disconnect between scholarship and commonly held religious beliefs.

While modern theology offers new insights, it also asks new questions. I hope you will find your own answers and begin to question — to question the answers others give you — and to question my opinions as well. Beyond that, I hope you will learn to *question the questions* that others think they are answering for you. If the questions are irrelevant, so are the answers.

This book is about questions — questions to explore Jesus and his message.

I use the Bible and other ancient documents as my primary sources. These documents are not histories in the modern sense, but they are part of a historical record; and they must be interpreted and evaluated according to specific rules. My rules have been placed in Appendix B. You may disagree with them and have your own, but you cannot *competently* interpret historical documents with no rules at all. If you find sources that contradict each other, it is not sufficient simply to choose one over the other. Competence demands that one make decisions based on logic and methodology.

To avoid bias as much as possible, it is necessary to use the most reliable and complete data available and to use it logically. Even when this task is complete, we must still ask more questions and seek better answers.

CHAPTER 1

# Historical and Cultural Context

We begin with the backdrop of the Bible, Jesus and his message.

## The Physical World

The Hebrew world had three levels:

1) The earth on which we live was in the middle or second tier.
2) Below the earth was the world of the dead and of evil spirits, variously called limbo, Hades, hell, or other names.
3) Above the earth was heaven or the heavenly realm, the home of God, the angels and heavenly beings.

On earth we are separated from hell by the ground or the sea. We are separated from heaven by the *firmament*, which is a *solid* sky. The creation of the firmament is described in Genesis 1:7, when, on the second day of creation, there was water all around the earth, both below and above; God then slipped in the firmament, like a dome or upside-down fish bowl, over the earth to divide the waters above from the waters below. The Hebrews imagined that when God wanted to send rain, port holes would be opened in the firmament to let the waters above fall to the ground. The stars were fixed or fastened into the sky, and in some cultures they were thought to be living beings.

The Jews retained this three-tiered image of the world in the first century. At Jesus' baptism Luke says that heaven was *opened* and the holy spirit descended upon him.[1] Matthew says that the heavens were *opened* to Jesus and he saw the spirit descend like a dove.[2] In each case there was a hole opening in the firmament or sky, enabling the spirit to pass through or someone to see into heaven.

John of Patmos employs similar imagery in Revelation 19:11, when he sees the heavens opened. In Revelation 4:1 he is able to see into heaven when a *door was open*.

## God

Judaism is credited with advocating monotheism, the belief in only one god, in the midst of a polytheistic world. This was not so in the beginning of Israel's history. Throughout the Old Testament there are numerous signs that the Hebrew religious mind embraced henotheism, a belief in one god among many others. At certain periods of history the God of Israel may have been worshiped along with a consort.

The Israelites had numerous names for God; unlike Christians, "Creator" or "Maker" was seldom used. In the early stages of the development of Christianity, many debated how the world came into being. The result was the Christian doctrine of creation out of nothing. This view is found in the first lesson in the *Baltimore Catechism*:

> 1. Who made us?
> God made us.
> *In the beginning, God created heaven and earth. (Genesis 1:1)*

From the quotation of Genesis 1:1, the act of creation is the beginning of the existence of all things. The belief in creation out of nothing is an assumption underlying the question.

The quotation of Genesis 1:1 is probably the one most familiar to Christian Bible readers. It is not, however, the most accurate. The New Revised Standard Version translates this verse as "In the beginning when

---

1 Luke 3:21
2 Matthew 3:16

God created..." But if you read the NRSV footnote, you will find an alternate translation, "When God began to create..." This latter formula seems to be the preferred translation among Jewish scholars, and does *not* support creation out of nothing.

In the Old Testament God is sometimes described as war-like and cruel, ordering the slaughter of whole tribes, including women and children. In these stories the authors interpreted events as they perceived them. We must not interpret their perceptions as historical facts.

## Human Nature

Genesis describes God forming the first man out of the dust of the earth and breathing into him the breath of life.[3] This is the typical view of human nature in the Bible. A human being has two parts, a material body and the breath of life. In both Hebrew and Greek the word we translate as spirit has breath as its basic meaning. It also meant wind, imagined as a giant breath. For the Hebrews you had to have both body and soul (or spirit or breath) to be a human being. The Jews did not in their early history believe in life after death. The book of Daniel was the first to postulate a resurrection of the body.

This belief had repercussions in Christian theology. Gnostic Christians after the first century believed that they could experience the risen Jesus directly and spiritually, independently of the hierarchy of bishops and priests. The bishops, who were the predecessors of the Catholic hierarchy, reacted by insisting that the only true experiencers of the risen Christ were those who witnessed his physical resurrection. To be in union with Christ, it was necessary to accept the authority of the bishops, who were the successors of those who witnessed the (bodily) resurrection.

The resurrection of the body is a fundamental doctrine in the Apostles' Creed and other creeds as well. The Catholic Church still teaches that we will get our bodies back at the end of time, and Pope Pius

---

3   Genesis 2:7

XII taught that God creates each human soul at the moment of conception. Therefore we have one life to live, with the specific body and soul we have in this life. When we die we become incomplete persons, which will be remedied only at the resurrection of the dead.

At times we find indications of different beliefs. For instance, Jesus says that "[John the Baptist] is Elijah who is to come."[4] The belief in the return of Elijah was widespread, and some interpret Jesus' words as indicating that John was the reincarnation of Elijah. According to Epiphanius, the Ebionites (Jewish followers in the second century C.E. and later) believed that Jesus was the incarnation of an archangel.

## Children of Abraham

In 586 B.C.E. the Babylonians destroyed the Temple of Solomon and the city of Jerusalem, and deported all the leading Jews. Thus began the exile, which ended when Cyrus the Great of Persia conquered Babylonia and allowed the Jews to return in 539 B.C.E. Within the next ten to twenty years the former exiles had rebuilt the temple.

The leader of the rebuilding project was Nehemiah, a Jewish official in the Persian court. As construction proceeded, Ezra the scribe arrived with authority from Persia to reestablish the Jewish law, thereby initiating a spiritual renewal.

Because of his mission, we would expect that Ezra would have set out to enforce all aspects of the Torah. And yet, in the books of Nehemiah and Ezra, the only reform recorded was to assure pure bloodlines among the Jews. Israelites who had survived exile from the Northern Kingdom were cast out of this new community of Jews, because their bloodlines traceable to Abraham were doubtful. And for the first time in Israel's history those Jews who had remained in the land and had married wives of a different race or religion were commanded to dismiss their wives and children.

---

4   Matthew 11:14

The strict enforcement of racial purity and the necessity of being able to prove one's Abrahamitic ancestry gave birth to the attitude prevalent among first-century Jews, that they were superior because Abraham was their father. Beginning with Nehemiah and Ezra, Jews had to document the purity of their bloodline.

## The Son of Man and the Apocalyptic World View

John the Baptist and Jesus both voiced a widely held theological view called apocalypticism, which had earlier appeared in the Old Testament book of Daniel. At the beginning of this book, it seems that we are reading the autobiographical account of a Jewish prophet who lived when Nebuchadnezzar destroyed Jerusalem in 586 B.C.E. However, the author gives clues that this is not the case.

In Daniel 1:1, Nebuchadnezzar conquers Jerusalem in the *third* year of the reign of Judah's king Jehoiakim. *The problem:* Jehoiakim reigned not for three years but for eleven, and Nebuchadnezzar conquered Jerusalem in the *first* year of the reign of Jehoiachin, the *son* of Jehoiakim.

And in Daniel 5:30, Belshazzar, the Chaldean king, is killed, and the kingdom falls to Darius the Mede, who is sixty-two years old. *The problem:* it was Cyrus the Persian who conquered Babylon in 539 B.C.E. Darius was not a Mede but a Persian, and he succeeded Cambyses, son of Cyrus, in 521 B.C.E.

Any Hebrew writing in 586 B.C.E. would not have made such clumsy mistakes. Hence the author of Daniel only *pretended* to write in the sixth century B.C.E.

The author of First Maccabees mentions Daniel in 2:60. When he refers to the "abomination of desolation" in Daniel 1:54, he is disparaging the act of Antiochus Epiphanes IV in setting up a statue of Zeus in the temple in 167 B.C.E. Daniel, then, had to be written after that date.

Daniel predicts the death of the one responsible for the abomination of desolation[5] as taking place "between the sea and the beautiful

---

5   Daniel 11:45

holy mountain." This fuzzy prediction says that Antiochus would die somewhere between the Mediterranean and Jerusalem. The author must have thought the odds were in his favor to have this prediction come true. Unfortunately for him, Antiochus died in Persia. Since Daniel was wrong about the location of Antiochus's death, he must have finished his book before 164 B.C.E, the year Antiochus died.

Most authorities agree that the book was written between 167 and 164 BCE. The prophet Daniel, then, is not a historical figure. Nor does the book relate historical facts. Jews who knew their history and read the book at the time it was written would have recognized the message and symbolism in it and would not have taken it literally.

For the past fifty years or so many Scripture scholars have believed that Daniel belongs to *apocalyptic* literature. Although such literature was widespread in the few centuries before and after Jesus' birth, the Bible has only two books belonging to this category: Daniel and Revelation. These are some characteristics of this kind of literature:

1) It is colorful and symbolic, often confusing, but understandable to Jewish readers. Often it is told as one or more visions.

2) The view of the world is dualistic, sharply dividing good and evil. On the side of good is God with the angels, and evil is seen as a cosmic power or personified as Satan or as one or more evil spirits.

3) Because the cosmic power of evil is in control, apocalypticism is pessimistic about the present. There is no way to escape from the dominion of evil until God intervenes.

4) Apocalyptic literature is crisis literature. Written in a time of oppression, it attempts to console the reader with a message of God's *imminent intervention* in history to reward the good and punish the wicked. It is *an attempt to solve the problem of evil* in a world where the good often suffer and the evil often enjoy life. God's immediate intervention may signal the beginning of the end of time, or end times, which are depicted as coming soon, not in the distant future.

5) Finally, since the author knows all about his own time but nothing about what is to come, those who attempt to read this literature as predicting the future are forced to make constant revisions in their prophecies as time passes.

Daniel was written when Antiochus Epiphanes IV placed a statue of Zeus in the Jerusalem temple and had outlawed Jewish religion. The book encouraged the Jews to uphold their religion and be steadfast in facing persecution, with trust that God would overcome their enemies in the end.

The vision of Daniel pictures various beasts representing nations that warred against Israel up to and including the time of Antiochus Epiphanes. The son of man, consequently, would represent the *nation of Israel*, which was to overcome evil in the world. Over time the son of man was imagined to be *an individual* who would represent Israel in conquering evil with God's power.

## The Forced Conversion of Galilee

In 167 B.C.E. the Greek King Antiochus IV Epiphanes outlawed Jewish religion and customs, while dedicating the Jerusalem temple to the Greek god Zeus. This was the notorious abomination of desolation spoken of in Daniel, and it touched off the Maccabean revolt, which resulted in the rescission of the hated edict by Antiochus V and the rededication of the temple. The rebellion, however, continued under the same family and their successors, known as the Hasmoneans.

The land of Judah, which at that time was just a small area in the center of what is now Israel, thus gained its independence and freedom to practice its religion and customs. In 134 B.C.E., John Hyrcanus I began his reign by expanding the kingdom. He conquered Idumea to the south, as well as Samaria and parts of Transjordan. However, the revolutionary movement which began as a pursuit of religious freedom did not share its quest for tolerance under the rule of the Hasmoneans. John Hyrcanus destroyed the Samaritan temple on Mt. Gerizim, and he allowed the

Gentile Idumaeans to remain in their homes only if they were circumcised and practiced Judaism. With little choice, the Idumaeans converted.

In 104 B.C.E. John Hyrcanus was succeeded by his son, Aristobulus, who quickly conquered the southern part of Iturea and the Golan to the north. The conquered portion of Iturea became known as Galilee. Aristobulus continued the policies of his father by allowing the inhabitants of Galilee to remain in their homes only if they converted to Judaism. The result was a population of Gentile converts with possibly a few settlers from Judea or elsewhere.

This shows why many Jews objected to a messiah coming from Galilee. At the time of Jesus the native population could trace their Jewish roots back only about a hundred thirty years. Before that time all their ancestors had been Gentiles, and true Galileans could lay no claim to being descendants of David or of Abraham, and the messiah and king of Israel had to be descendants of Abraham. Galileans were, of course, *religious* Jews, but they were not *ethnic* Jews (i.e., belonging to the Jewish race). All Jews knew that the people in Galilee were not descendants of Abraham.

## The Jewish View of Pagans and Proselytes

"Proselytes" is the name given to Gentiles who fully converted to Judaism, which for males included circumcision. They were real Jews, and some became noted teachers. They were not, however, equal to other Jews (descendants of Abraham). Women proselytes could not marry a priest unless converted before the age of three. Children of a proselyte could not inherit from their father if they were born before the proselyte's conversion. After the destruction of the Temple, a proselyte was regarded as without father, mother or any other relationship. There were also restrictions on the right to hold some civic offices, such as in the Sanhedrin.[6]

---

6   Jeremias, Joachim, *Jerusalem in the Time of Jesus,* Fortress Press, Philadelphia, 1975, pages 320-354.

Jews of Abrahamitic origin could claim a share in the merits of their ancestors; proselytes could not. Ethnic Jews were made acceptable to God by the prayers and merits of their forefathers, especially of Abraham. Through ancestral prayers and merits they were able to appease God, make up for punishment for their sins, and be guaranteed a place in the eternal kingdom of God. Proselytes, on the other hand, were on their own: if they fell into sin, they had to get back into God's favor without the spiritual help of ancestors guaranteed to ethnic Jews.[7]

From the way Jews regarded proselytes we can see what they thought of Gentiles. A proselyte had no father or mother, because Jews believed that Gentiles so lacked sexual morality that all Gentiles were to be treated as illegitimate. It was impossible to avoid all association with them, but the Jews saw evil so prevalent in pagan society that not only was intermarriage forbidden, but so was eating with them. The worship of false gods put them under the power of evil, a cosmic power in control of the world or personified as an evil spirit.

---

7   *Ibid.*

CHAPTER 2

# A Divided Christianity

At the end of the first century C.E., a man named John composed the book of Revelation on the island of Patmos. He began by addressing seven churches in Asia Minor, now Turkey. To each church he quotes what he says Jesus told him to write. For two of them, Pergamum[8] and Thyatira,[9] he condemned their practice of eating food sacrificed to idols.

For John, eating such food was always offensive to God, and he placed the prohibition on the lips of Jesus in a vision. However, what John *condemned* without reservation, the apostle Paul explicitly *allowed* in First Corinthians 8.

Both John and Paul backed up their position with personal visions of the risen Jesus; at the same time, they contradicted each other.

John also opposed those who claimed to be Jews but were not. It is easy to see how this attitude arose among Paul's converts, who were likely among the predecessors of those to whom John was writing. They were able to reject circumcision while at the same time claiming to be heirs of Christ under a "new covenant." Paul rejected the attitude of superiority of Gentiles over Jews, but by the second century many Gentile Christians had become anti-Semitic.

---

8   Revelation 2:14
9   Revelation 2:20

In Acts, Luke smoothed over the arguments between Paul and the Jerusalem community. John of Patmos, in adopting the position of the Jewish followers in the early Jerusalem church, must have been a Jewish follower of Jesus, and his absolute condemnation of what Paul allowed tells us that the divisions between the apostles in Jerusalem and Paul were never healed.

The dispute over eating food offered to idols was just one of the many splits that emerged by the end of the first century. In the epistles of First and Second John we find references to a novel idea that was gaining a significant following. The author condemns those who say that Jesus did not come in the flesh, i.e., that he did not have a physical body. He called these people "antichrists," but today they are called Docetists, from a Greek word *dokeo*, meaning to appear or to seem. The Docetists believed that Jesus only seemed to have a human body, and therefore he only appeared to suffer and die.

By the end of the second century Irenaeus, bishop of Lyons, wrote a five-volume work *Against Heresies*, or *Adversus Haereses*, describing over a dozen heretical beliefs. The word "heresy" in Greek meant "choice," so that Irenaeus was writing against all choices in doctrine except what he himself believed. He made correct belief essential to being an authentic Christian. Those who disagreed with him were heretics, and in Chapter XXVII of Book V he described how believers will be separated from unbelievers at the time of judgment. Of course, all those heretics he condemned thought that only they had correct belief, and that all other Christians were heretics.

Why were the early Christians so deeply divided? This question can be divided into two parts: *1) Why couldn't Christians agree on what Jesus taught? 2) Why couldn't those who succeeded the apostles correct those in error and unify Christians?*

I will address these questions and the assumptions behind them in the next two sections.

## A. Christian Belief

While many of the details related as historical in the Gospels may be uncertain, there is less dispute about what Jesus taught. In the Sermon on the Mount in Matthew, we find the beatitudes and commands about anger, oaths, adultery, charitable giving and prayer, including the Lord's Prayer. Luke gives the same teachings in different words, along with lessons on God's mercy, as in the parable of the prodigal son. Jesus' exact words may be lost, but we least know how the first believers understood his message.

The turning point for the disciples was the resurrection, which forced the disciples to change their theological perspective. God had raised Jesus from the dead and made him Lord and Messiah. Jesus had conquered sin and death, but this was a personal victory, and his followers had yet to figure out how — and how much — they were to share in that victory. The kingdom of God in its fullness was still to come, and it would be heralded by the second coming of Jesus.

The disciples changed their perspective of time. They were suddenly living in the "in between" time, the time between the *initial coming* of God's kingdom (with the resurrection) and its *final day* when Jesus would return. This "in between" time would be brief, and early on it must have seemed that they did not have much time to spread their message. The Acts of the Apostles relates how the Twelve struggled to carry this out, turning first to their own people and then to the Gentiles.

Before long, the message of the apostles grew into a multitude of opposing opinions. To answer our first question, *why couldn't Christians agree on what Jesus taught*, we will start by looking at one belief on which nearly every Christian agreed, at least through most of the first century, and that is the immediate return of Jesus. This belief was a continuation of the message of John the Baptist.

### The Apocalyptic Message of John the Baptist

In all four Gospels John was baptizing and preaching before Jesus began his ministry. Matthew gives a summary of his message:

> ⁷But when John saw many Pharisees and Sadducees coming for baptism, he said to them, "You brood of snakes! Who warned you to run away from the coming wrath? ⁸Bear good works that show true repentance. ⁹Do not be presumptuous and say to yourselves, 'Our father is Abraham.' Let me tell you, God can raise up children for Abraham from these stones. ¹⁰And right now the ax is placed at the root of the trees; therefore every tree that does not produce good fruit is going to be cut down and tossed into the fire."[10]

This is a warning of an imminent judgment in which God will overthrow the power of evil and punish those who do not repent of their sins.

## Jesus' Apocalyptic Message

Jesus, like John, preached an apocalyptic message. His theme in the Synoptic Gospels (Matthew, Mark and Luke) is the coming of the kingdom of God. He called on all to repent or to change their way of thinking *at once*, because the kingdom of God was at hand and God was going to immediately overturn the world order in which evil had control. The first will be last and the last, first. And when will this happen? Jesus said soon, even in the lifetimes of some who heard him:

> ¹And [Jesus] said to them, "Amen (Indeed) I say to you, there are some standing here who will not taste death until they see the kingdom of God coming in power."[11]

This saying is considered authentic, since the early Christians would not have invented a prediction that had failed to come to pass.

Jesus is also clear on what was in store for the Twelve:

> ²⁷Then Peter said [to Jesus], "Behold, we have left everything and followed you. So what are we going to have?"
>
> ²⁸Jesus answered, "Amen (Indeed) I tell you, when everything is renewed and the son of man is seated on his glorious throne, you

---

10  Matthew 3:7-10
11  Mark 9:1

who have followed me will also sit on twelve thrones, judging the twelve tribes of Israel."[12]

These words, too, can be traced to Jesus himself. Early Christians would not have made up such a promise that included Judas.

The kingdom of God was going to happen right away and on earth. God was going to make the last first and the first last, *in the immediate here and now*, overturning the world order, eliminating the reign of evil and sin in the world, and restoring God's reign *on earth*. It was only after Christians realized that Jesus was not going to come right away, that they began to think of God's kingdom as something far in the future and only after we die. (When we pray, "Thy kingdom come," we are still praying for God to come soon and eliminate evil in this world.)

## Paul's Apocalyptic Message

Paul taught the same apocalyptic message, explaining how those who are still living when Jesus comes will not have an advantage over those who have died. "The Lord himself…will descend from heaven." Then the dead will rise first, and the living will meet Christ in the air together with them, to be with the Lord forever.

> [13]However. brothers and sisters, we do not want you to be ignorant about those who are sleeping [in the grave], so that you may not be sorrowful like those without hope. [14]For if we believe that Jesus died and resurrected, likewise, those who have fallen asleep through Jesus, God will bring forth with him.
>
> [15]For we state this to you in the word of the Lord, that we who are living, who are still here at the coming of the Lord, will not go ahead of those who have fallen asleep. [16]For the Lord himself, with a resounding command, with a call from the archangel and with the blare of God's trumpet, will descend from heaven, and the dead in Christ will rise first. [17]Then we who are alive, who are still here, will be snatched up in the clouds together with them to

---

12  Matthew 19:27-28. The words "son of man" are not capitalized in the Greek.

meet the Lord in the air; and thus we will be with the Lord forever. ¹⁸Therefore console each other with these words.[13]

## Other Apocalyptic Writers

Other New Testament writers expressed the same belief: Encourage one another… "as you see the Day approaching."[14] And John of Patmos has Jesus repeatedly saying, "I am coming soon."[15]

The *Didache (The Teaching of the Twelve Apostles)*, written probably between 100 and 120 C.E., about ten to thirty years after Revelation, was still looking forward to the coming of the Lord, although the expectation was no longer immediate.[16]

## How the Apocalyptic Outlook Changed

The apocalyptic message of Jesus and John the Baptist was preserved beyond the end of the first century, but it was changed by Jesus' followers. The way it was changed is the key to our question, *why couldn't the early Christians agree on what Jesus taught?*

At the time of Jesus' death and resurrection, the disciples remembered Jesus' promises right up to the time of the crucifixion, in expectation of the immediate coming of God's kingdom. They were also anticipating being seated on the twelve thrones to judge the twelve tribes of Israel.[17]

The apostles may have thought that Jesus was the Messiah, but Jesus did not fit the messianic image of most Jews, which was of someone who would triumphantly liberate Israel from all foreign domination and reign as king.

Right after the crucifixion, the apostles would have been confused and disillusioned, thinking only of the loss of their leader. They ques-

---

13  First Thessalonians 4:13-18
14  Hebrews 10:25
15  Revelation 3:11, 22:12, 22:20
16  *Didache,* Chapters 10:6, 16:7-8
17  Matthew 19:27-28

tioned whether they had been wrong about who Jesus was and what he had promised.

The resurrection changed this. We do not know what the disciples experienced, since the resurrection narratives in the Gospels conflict with each other; but whatever their experience was, they believed that Jesus had returned from the dead.

We have a clue to their thinking from the Acts of the Apostles. According to Luke, the first apostolic message was that God *made* Jesus the Messiah by *raising* him from the dead.[18] This terminology may be a genuine reflection of how the gospel was first preached, since it differs from other New Testament passages saying that Jesus *rose* (not "was raised). In Acts Jesus does not rise on his own as later formulations state, but God *raised* him. Also, it is the resurrection that turns Jesus into the Messiah. Later on Christians thought of Jesus as becoming the Messiah at his baptism or being proclaimed Messiah at the time of his birth.

## Jesus Seen as the Son of Man

As the resurrection receded into the past, the view of time and of the final age had to change. The arrival of the kingdom was further and further out of sight, and followers of Jesus looked forward less to a new kingdom and more to Jesus' *second* coming. Jesus then became the prophet Daniel's "son of man" who was to come on the clouds in majesty.

Whether Jesus believed that he himself was this "son of man" is doubtful. The expression "son of man" is used often in the Gospels as another way to say "man" or "human being," as well as to refer to the "son of man" from the book of Daniel. There are some passages in the Gospels where Jesus refers to himself as the coming "son of man," and others that are ambiguous, leaving us in doubt whether it refers to the "son of man" in Daniel or simply to himself. However, some sayings indicate that Jesus originally taught that the "son of man" was someone else. For example,

---

18  Acts 2:32,36

> [38]"For whoever is ashamed of me and of my message in this adulterous and sinful generation, of that one the son of man will likewise be ashamed when he will come in the glory of his Father with the holy angels."[19]
>
> [8]"But I tell you, everyone who professes me before others, the son of man will also profess before the angels of God; [9]but whoever rejects me before others will be rejected before the angels of God.
>
> [10]And whoever speaks something against the son of man will be forgiven; but whoever shall have blasphemed against the holy spirit will not be forgiven."[20]
>
> [27]"For the son of man is going to come in the glory of his Father with his angels, and then he will render to each one according to one's works. [28]Amen I say to you, there are some standing here who will not taste death until they see the son of man coming in his kingdom."[21]

In these passages Jesus talks about the "son of man" in the third person, while at the same time referring to himself in first person. A switch from first to third person indicates a reference to someone other than oneself.

Besides the titles of "Messiah" and "Son of Man," Jesus acquired another title by the end of the first century. In Mark a centurion, upon Jesus' death, exclaims, "Truly this man was a son of God."[22] In this context "son of God" did not infer divinity, but was the equivalent of a just man, a holy man, or a man chosen or loved by God. John the evangelist changed the meaning of these words and elevated Jesus to the "Son of God" who was divine and equal to the Father. This is the title that took precedence in later generations.

---

19  Mark 8:38. The words "son of man" are not capitalized in the Greek.
20  Luke 12:8-10. The words "son of man" and "holy spirit" are not capitalized in the Greek.
21  Matthew 16:27-28. The words "son of man" are not capitalized in the Greek.
22  Mark 15:39

*False Questions*

## Interpretations of Jesus and His Crucifixion

The conviction about Jesus' messsiahship was problematic for the first generation of followers. Jesus had to be sinless, so why was he subject to such ignominy and torture, and crucified as a public criminal? Of the various opinions on this question, the solution of Paul was the one that prevailed. Paul reasoned that since Jesus did not die for his own sins, he must have died for the sins of others. This is the theology of vicarious redemption, in which Jesus died as a sacrifice to atone for the sins of all mankind. For his sacrifice to be adequate, it had to have infinite or divine love — or the love of a divine being — behind it. This is one more reason for professing Jesus as divine.

The message of the witnesses to the resurrection was simple: Jesus was raised from the dead and became the Messiah. He died for the sins of all. To be saved from sin one must accept Jesus. The time is short, because he will return soon.

This outline of apostolic teaching left much to be explained, and Christians created numerous explanations and amplifications on every aspect. Here are a few of the many Christian churches which developed their own versions of the message:

*Docetism*: Jesus' body was an illusion.

*Monophysitism*: Christ's divinity completely overtook his humanity, resulting in one divine-human nature.

*Monotheletism*: Jesus had two natures, but only one will.

*Sabellianism*: The Father, Son and Holy Spirit are three modes of the divinity and not three distinct persons.

*Adoptionism*: Jesus was adopted as God's son when the Spirit descended upon him. The *Ebionites* were adoptionists, who, also believed (according to Epiphanius) that Jesus was the incarnation of an archangel.

*Apollinarism*: Jesus had a human body and emotions, but a divine mind.

*Marcionism*: There are two gods: the wrathful god of the Old Testament and the merciful Father of Jesus. Marcion, its founder, created the first canon or list of approved scripture, which included most of the writings of Paul and the Gospel of Luke, which he edited.

*Gnosticism*: This belief had many versions. It was dualistic, teaching that spirits or souls were trapped in an evil, material world. It emphasized union with the risen Christ through one's personal spiritual experience rather than being subject to the bishop's authority and teaching.

*Arianism*: Named after Arius but taught before his time, it professed that Jesus was only human and not divine.

From the first century until the fourth, Christians argued over who Jesus was — only a man, only God, a being who only appeared to be a man, a man with the Christ (consciousness) or divinity present from his baptism to his crucifixion, or both God and man. This dispute was not settled until the Council of Nicea in 325 C.E.

## Our Answer

We can now answer our question, *why couldn't early Christians agree on what Jesus taught?* Behind this question is the false assumption that they were very much concerned about what he taught. Instead, they argued, often vehemently, about who Jesus was and why he had to be crucified. *Jesus had become the message, and the message he preached became secondary.* What Jesus taught was tossed aside in favor of dogmas that are nowhere in his message.

## B. Christian Authority

Between 313 and 340 C.E., Eusebius, bishop of Caesarea in Palestine, wrote a ten-volume work titled *Church History*. As the first such work ever undertaken, it provided the framework for the Christian view of history for centuries. Living after Christians won a favored status under Constantine, Eusebius wrote from the vantage point of the Catholic Church, which in the Council of Nicea in 325 C.E. had won the war over rival churches. Beginning with the teaching of Arius, who taught that Jesus Christ was a human being but not divine, the teachings of opposing Christian communities were stamped out and their writings were destroyed. The Catholic Church became the winner over paganism and other Christian communities, and the historical view of Eusebius became the winner as well.

What Eusebius taught in his *Church History* eventually became encapsulated in the standard defense of the Catholic Church called apologetics, a course summarized in catechisms and taught in seminaries. This theological view of history is summarized as follows:

> *Jesus Christ promised to build his church upon Simon Peter and to give him the keys to the kingdom in Matthew 16:18-19. He also gave Peter and the other apostles the power to bind and loose in heaven whatever they bound and loosed here on earth in Matthew 16:19 and 18:18. The apostles handed on their spiritual power and authority by the laying on of hands, and those who received this power became bishops. Peter became the first bishop of Rome, and those who succeeded him as bishops of Rome had authority over all other Christian churches.*

If this view of history is correct, then we have to answer the second question, *why couldn't those who succeeded the apostles correct those in error and unify Christians?*

## The Authority Given to the Apostles

On whether Jesus gave his twelve apostles any unique powers or authority, Luke has the following:

> ¹Jesus called together the twelve and gave them power and authority over all demons, and to cure diseases. ²He sent them out to proclaim the kingdom of God and to heal the sick. ³He said to them, "Take nothing for your mission, not a staff, nor a bag, nor bread, nor money, nor more than one coat. ⁴When you enter a family's home, stay as their guest until you leave for the next village. ⁵As for those who do not receive you, shake off all the dust from your feet as testimony against them." ⁶They left and walked through the villages, proclaiming the good news and healing everywhere.
>
> ...
>
> [After they returned,]
>
> ⁴⁹John answered, "Master, we saw someone casting out demons in your name, and we demanded that he stop, because he does not follow as one of us."
>
> ⁵⁰But Jesus replied, "No, do not stop him, because those who are not against you are for you."[23]

Chapter 9 of Luke begins with Jesus giving the Twelve the power to cast out demons and to cure diseases. This may have been a single power, since many at the time believed that illness was caused by evil spirits. After they returned, John tells Jesus that someone outside their circle was also casting out demons in his name, and that they ordered him to stop. Jesus' reply indicates that the unknown man, though not commissioned or authorized by Jesus, had the same power and authority as that given to the Twelve.[24] Hence the apostles, even if given special power, could not claim that it was exclusive to them.

---

23  Luke 9:1-6, 49-50
24  To avoid confusion, I will at times refer the apostles chosen by Jesus as "the Twelve," since others were also called apostles in the first century.

Jesus is also said to give the Twelve the power to bind and loose:

> [15]"If your brothers or sisters sin against you, go and tell them their fault between you and them alone. If they listen, then you have won them back. [16]But if they will not listen, approach them again with one or two others, so that all that is said may be held up by the testimony of two or three witnesses. [17]And if they refuse to listen to your group, then tell the community. But if they refuse even to listen to the church, then consider them the same as a [non believing] Gentile or as a [cheating] tax collector.
>
> [18]"Amen, I tell you, whatever you bind on earth will be bound in heaven, and whatever you unbind on earth will be unbound in heaven.
>
> [19]"Again I tell you that if two of you on earth agree on anything you ask for, it will be done for you by my Father in heaven. [20]For where two or three are gathered together in my name, there I am with them."
>
> [21]Then Peter came to him and said, "If my brother or sister sins against me, how many times should I forgive? Up to seven times?" [22]Jesus said to him, "I wouldn't say seven times, but seventy times seven times."[25]

This passage is used by Matthew to segue into Jesus' parable of the unforgiving servant, and was used in the early church as the basis for the power to forgive its members. It begins with a short instruction that some Bibles label "Fraternal Correction," explaining how to correct those in the community who have committed a serious crime. First, you talk to them privately. If there is no change in behavior, you confront the guilty parties along with two or three others. If your conversations are still fruitless, you bring your charges to the whole community. And if they refuse to listen to the community, then the community binds them by ostracizing them and treating them like Gentiles or tax collectors.

Ejection from the community is what Paul orders the Corinthians to do to the man guilty of incest in First Corinthians 5:1-5.

---

25  Matthew 18:15-22

The community also had the power to loose (or unbind), which is the authority to forgive guilty but repentant persons by receiving them back into their community. This is what Paul commands the Corinthians to do to the guilty party in Second Corinthians 2:5-11. By welcoming sinners, the church is exercising the power to loose or forgive.

Early Christians had no practice of confession or sacrament of reconciliation. In the first few centuries, Christian churches used the power of binding and loosing, which was the power to punish and to forgive; the power to bind came to be called excommunication, the practice of refusing communion. Forgiveness was exercised by letting someone return to communion. But we must not overextend this power of forgiveness: The community had the power to loose what the community *had itself bound,* to forgive by removing a penalty the community *had itself imposed.* The story of Jesus giving the power to bind and to loose segues into his insistence on forgiving over and over, which is illustrated by the parable of the unforgiving servant.

Matthew 18 tells us that the Twelve must not tolerate sin among themselves or among the larger number of disciples, but must be willing to forgive again and again.

## Peter's Primacy

Finally, what are we to make of Peter's privilege?

> [13]When Jesus came into Caesarea Philippi, he asked his disciples, "Who are people saying that the son of man is?"
>
> [14]And they replied, "Some are saying John the Baptist; some, Elijah; and some, Jeremiah or one of the prophets."
>
> [15]He said to them, "But who do you say that I am?"
>
> [16]Simon Peter replied, "You are the Messiah, the son of the living God."
>
> [17]Jesus answered, "You can be glad, Simon, son of Jonah, because flesh and blood has not revealed this to you, but my Father in heaven.

> ¹⁸And I say to you, you are Peter, and on this rock I will build my church, and the gates of hell will not prevail against it.
>
> ¹⁹And I will give you the keys of the kingdom of heaven, and whatever you bind on earth will be bound in heaven, and whatever you loose on earth will be loosed in heaven."
>
> ²⁰Then he commanded the disciples not to tell anyone else that he was the Messiah.[26]

In this passage Peter is given the keys of the kingdom, explained as the same power to bind and to loose which was given to the Twelve. The words used to affirm the primacy of Peter over all Christians are from verse 18, "And I say to you, you are Peter, and on this rock I will build my church, and the gates of hell will not prevail against it."

Catholic apologetics explains Matthew 16 in this way:

> *Jesus gives this apostle a new name, Peter, which means "Rock." Although Peter is a masculine noun and the Greek word for rock, petra, is feminine, it is clear that Peter is the rock upon which the church of Jesus would be built. And so we have not only Jesus' express intention to establish a church, but also to make Peter its head.*
>
> *When Jesus says that the gates of hell will not prevail against his church, he is promising that it will endure until the end of time.*
>
> *There is historical information to say that Peter was martyred and buried in Rome, so that he became the first bishop of Rome. Those who followed Peter as bishop of Rome had the same office as Peter and became the head of the church established by Jesus. Later on the bishop of Rome came to have the title of pope.*

---

26  Matthew 16:13-20. The titles "son of man" and "son of the living God" use capitals only for the word for God in the Greek.

This argument misuses the word for *church*. The Greek word for church is *ekklesía,* derived from a Greek verb that means "to call" or "to call out." In the biblical concordance *ekklesía* is defined as "that which is called out." The first followers of Jesus called their communities churches, since it meant that they had been called.

The Catholic interpretation of Matthew 16 gives the Greek word for church a meaning it could *never* have had: *a (new) organized religion.* The use of the passage to prove that Jesus established a new religion with Peter as its head is reading *into* the text rather than reading what the author intended. After Jesus died, the Twelve remained a community of *Jews*, never abandoning Judaism.

The gates of hell do not refer to how long Jesus' church will endure, but only that evil will not harm it.

The leaders of Jesus' community are the Twelve, who are to judge not the Gentiles, but the twelve tribes of Israel. This is not a new organization outside Judaism, and it is to reach its fulfillment before some of those present taste death.[27]

> [27]Then Peter said [to Jesus], "Look, we have left everything and followed you. So what are we going to have?"
>
> [28]Jesus answered, "Amen (Indeed) I tell you, when everything is renewed and the son of man is seated on his glorious throne, you who have followed me will also sit on twelve thrones, judging the twelve tribes of Israel. [29]And everyone who has left houses or brothers or sisters or father or mother or children or land, for the sake of my name, will receive a hundredfold and inherit eternal life. [30]But many who are first [now] will be last [then], and the last will be first."[28]

The argument for the primacy of Peter makes him the leader of the Twelve. Was he in charge after Jesus died?

---

27  Mark 9:1
28  Matthew 19:27-30

## Leadership of the Twelve After the Resurrection

After the resurrection there was a new leader of the Twelve. But it was not Peter; nor even one of the Twelve, but James the Just, named as the brother of Jesus in Mark 6 and in Galatians 1. In Acts 15, which tells us of the Council of Jerusalem deciding how to deal with Gentile followers of Jesus, it was not Peter, but James, who said, "I have decided..."[29] After James was martyred around 62 C.E., the leadership of these Jewish followers of Jesus continued to be held by the descendants of Joseph and Mary, later called Ebionites. For these Jewish believers, leadership was transferred by inheritance rather than by the laying on of hands or ordination.[30]

What, then, was the role of Peter? He was probably martyred in Rome about the same time as Paul between 62 and 67 C.E. We do not know what he did there or when he arrived or if he was there more than once. At the end of Paul's letter to the Romans, written between the years 50 and 60, Paul greets some twenty-five plus persons in the Roman church, and there must have been others whom Paul did not know. It is surprising that Paul knows this many by name when they are in a church he had never visited. We know nothing of its origin, but it was apparently flourishing at least a decade before either Peter or Paul arrived.

If Peter was in Rome at the time Paul wrote to the Romans, Paul would have had no reason to give them his own exposition of Christian teaching; and it would be unthinkable for him to omit Peter's name from the list of those he greets in his letter. When Paul addresses his letter to the church in Rome, he is addressing the community and not a leader, indicating that the Roman church had no leader. Some of Peter's activities are mentioned in Acts, but we have no knowledge of what he did in Rome.

---

29  Acts 15:19

30  The Ebionites were a community of Jewish followers of Jesus. Their leaders had to be descendants of the family of Mary and Joseph. Eusebius calls them *desposynoi,* and these leaders existed until at least 318 C.E., when they sent a delegation to Sylvester, the bishop of Rome, requesting that their church be acknowledged as first in rank because of its bloodline. Sylvester ignored their request.

## First Letter of Clement

In my seminary course in apologetics, I learned that at the end of the first century, Clement, the bishop of Rome at the time, wrote what is called the First Letter of Clement to the Corinthians. The church in Corinth had, for unstated reasons, deposed their presbyters or elders. The letter gives numerous reasons why the Corinthians should reinstate them. After receiving the letter, the Corinthians put their elders back in office, thereby acknowledging the authority of the bishop of Rome over their church. I accepted this interpretation of First Clement — until I read the letter for myself.

We do not know who wrote the First Letter of Clement. The author's name is not mentioned in the letter, and, like the Gospels, it received its title long after it was written. It was common for letters written in this period, like those of Paul, to begin with a salutation stating who was writing and to whom. And First Clement does exactly that: "The Church of God which is at Rome to the Church of God which is at Corinth." The letter is from one community to another, and not from one person in charge to another.

First Clement never says why the Corinthians deposed their elders, but it gives numerous arguments why they should reinstate them. It is true that the Corinthians acceded to the request from the church in Rome, but in the many arguments the Roman church put forth, the letter claims no authority over Corinth. It is obvious that neither Rome nor Corinth, at the end of the first century, had yet developed an organizational structure in which there was one person in charge. First Clement was written in the name of a community, not of an administrator, and it was up to the whole Corinthian church to reinstate their elders, and not the decision of a single leader. First Clement never argues that the Corinthian church lacked authority to dismiss its elders.

## No Overseers in Paul's Churches

The same logic applies when we read the letters of Paul the apostle. In every epistle, he never addresses a single officer, but only a community. First Corinthians is an excellent example of the absence of anyone in charge when Paul was away. The community was in chaos, and if someone had been overseeing the church, he would have addressed that person instead of the whole church. Paul had not appointed a successor in any of the communities he established, and he had no reason to do so. He was convinced that Jesus would return in his lifetime, as we learn First Thessalonians:

> [13]However. brothers and sisters, we do not want you to be ignorant about those who are sleeping (in the grave), so that you may not be sorrowful like those without hope. [14]For if we believe that Jesus died and resurrected, likewise, those who have fallen asleep through Jesus, God will bring forth with him. [15]For we state this to you in the word of the Lord, that we who are living, who are still here at the coming of the Lord, will not go ahead of those who have fallen asleep.
>
> [16]For the Lord himself, with a resounding command, with a call from the archangel and with the blare of God's trumpet, will descend from heaven, and the dead in Christ will rise first. [17]Then we who are alive, who are still here, will be snatched up in the clouds together with them to meet the Lord in the air; and thus we will be with the Lord forever. [18]Therefore console each other with these words.[31]

## The Pastoral Epistles

I was also taught that Paul addressed two church leaders whom he himself appointed, Timothy and Titus. In the Pastoral Epistles (First and Second Timothy and Titus) Paul not only writes directly to two church leaders, but also speaks of bishops, presbyters (elders) and deacons.

The problem is that Paul did not write these letters. The Pastoral Epistles contain 848 Greek words, of which over a third are not found in any of the other letters attributed to Paul, not even the Deuterocanonical (whose authorship is disputed) letters of Colossians, Ephesians and Second Thessalonians. And over ten percent of the words in the Pastoral Epistles are second century Greek vocabulary. Today these letters are commonly dated to the end of the first century at the earliest, at least a full generation after Paul was martyred.

---

31  First Thessalonians 4:13-18

Besides vocabulary, there are other reasons to say that the Pastoral Epistles are forgeries. For instance, the author uses the word for faith to mean a list of doctrines, and "faith" did not acquire this meaning until the second century. The author complains about those who profess a false knowledge of *gnosis,* and Gnosticism did not develop to this point until many decades after the time of Paul. Also, these letters are not listed with the writings of Paul by Marcion in his canon in the early second century. He either did not know of them or rejected them.

If the Catholic Church had known in the fourth century what we know now about the Pastoral Epistles, it would almost certainly have omitted them from the canon, as it did with the forged Third Corinthians.

## The Didache

One of the most important books outside the New Testament, is the *Didache* (pronounced *dee dah kay*) or the Teaching of the Apostles. Unlike most other documents of the time, the title of this work is part of the document itself. It could have been written as early as 100 C.E., and it may be a composite of several works. As the title suggests, the work claims to be a Christian manual of authentic teaching.

The Didache gives us relevant information on the development of a hierarchy among Christians. It tells how they relied on itinerant prophets who would visit, teach the people, celebrate the Eucharist (which may or may not have been a Last Supper ritual), then go on to another location. These wandering prophets were sometimes called apostles.

The document instructs Christian communities to elect for themselves bishops and deacons. These words meant overseers and attendants who serve the needs of others. Here we see that a form of clergy was developing. The members of a church would choose one group of persons to act as managers to oversee church business and perhaps worship, and another to be servants to act in a capacity similar to that of social workers. The church structure was in transition. We do not yet see a structure in which one person, such as a bishop, has authority over the whole community. From First Clement it is clear that the elected leaders were given their authority by the community and not by other leaders.

*False Questions*

A clerical hierarchy developed gradually in the latter decades of the first century and for some time into the second. At first churches selected elders (or presbyters), which may be what the Didache was talking about when speaking of overseers. This type of organization continued through the early part of the second century.

## Ignatius of Antioch

The first mention of an overseer or bishop as a single authority comes with Ignatius of Antioch around 110 C.E. He claimed to be bishop of all of Syria, but not everyone accepted him as such. In Philadelphia, where prophets were still honored as the primary authorities, Ignatius tried to win them over to accepting him as bishop by pretending to prophesy; he was roundly rejected.[32] In 110 C.E., then, the hierarchy of bishop, priest and deacon was still in a developmental stage.

Furthermore, the Gospels never imply that Jesus intended his teachings and movement to spread outside Judaism. Matthew explicitly says that Jesus came not to do away with the Law of Moses but to fulfill it, and in the Sermon on the Mount he is pictured as the new Moses or lawgiver. Jesus lived and died as a faithful Jew.

## Our Answer

Now we can answer our second question, *why couldn't those who succeeded the apostles correct those in error and unify Christians?* Underlying the question is a false assumption. The apostles never appointed successors. The Twelve never passed on any authority or power to anyone. The hierarchical structure with bishops at the top did not develop until sometime in the second century, and bishops today cannot claim to have received any spiritual power or authority from Jesus or the apostles. *Early Christians could not be unified, because there were no successors to the apostles with authority to unify them.*

---

32  Pagels, Elaine, *Revelations, Visions, Prophecy, & Politics in the Book of Revelation*, Viking, New York, 2012, pages 65-69.

CHAPTER 3

# Jesus as the Messiah

After the resurrection the disciples wanted to convince others that Jesus was Messiah and Lord. Few could accept what they had not experienced.

To believe an executed criminal was messiah was a stumbling block. It was not appealing to the Gentiles, but it was repulsive to the Jews. The popular Jewish image of the Messiah was of a glorified, conquering hero who would liberate Israel from foreign power. There were Jewish rebels who, both before and after Jesus' time, tried to fulfill that role, and none of them succeeded. Jesus ended his life in defeat without even trying to be a victorious liberator. Little wonder that he was utterly rejected.

The rejection of the disciples' claim was answered by an intense defense on the part of the first followers and the early Christians. In this chapter I will address the question, *how can we prove that Jesus was the promised Jewish Messiah?*

*False Questions*

# A. Jesus as the Son of David

When the disciples tried to persuade their fellow Jews that Jesus was the Messiah, they searched the Scriptures for prophecies that Jesus fulfilled. We find some of them in the infancy narratives.

Only Matthew and Luke tell the story of Jesus' birth. The images of these narratives, such as the Magi and the shepherds, are familiar. During the Christmas season Nativity sets pop up everywhere, and carols are sung on the radio around the clock. Believers and unbelievers alike know the story.

The nativity story does not fit into history. The central event, the virgin birth, like all miracles, can be accepted only on faith. The historian can say nothing about whether it really happened, but can only acknowledge its acceptance by believers.

Some have claimed the virgin birth to be an attempt to use pagan mythology to affirm the divinity of Jesus. This argument can be dismissed, since neither Gospel attempts to affirm his divinity.

Traditional Christian theology has defended the historicity of the Nativity narratives in Matthew and Luke. Theologians have pointed out that the two Gospels rely on independent sources that were not produced by collaboration, but do agree on important details. Among these details are these: Jesus grew up in Nazareth in Galilee; he was born in Bethlehem; Mary was his mother; Joseph was the head of the family, but not his father; Jesus was a descendant of King David.

## Contradictions with History

Churches have ignored the fact that many details in the stories cannot be reconciled, either with each other or with history. For example, Luke states that Jesus was born under the reign of Herod[33] *and* while Quirinius was governor of Syria.[34] Quirinius was indeed governor of Syria, but only *ten years after* the reign of Herod. Luke also relates that Joseph had to

---

33  Luke 1:5
34  Luke 2:1

go to Bethlehem because Augustus Caesar decreed a census. According to Luke, everyone had to return to one's ancestral home to be counted. There is no historical record of such a census, which would have caused chaos throughout the empire for everyone to leave one's home and go to who knows where. Historians today believe the census never happened.

Matthew's story is equally incredible. Astronomers have long tried to track down what star or comet could have led the Magi to Bethlehem. We have no record of such a celestial event in any writings of the time. If a star did appear over the house of Joseph and Mary, how could the Magi tell it was their house and not the one next door? A star directly over one house would appear to be directly over every house in every direction for miles around.

If Herod had ordered the slaughter of all children under two in Bethlehem or any city, someone should have written about it. He was responsible for the murder of his own son, so he was certainly capable of such an act. But without evidence, historians discount this event.

## Incompatibility of Matthew and Luke

Reading Matthew and Luke side by side reveals their incompatibility. For Luke, Joseph and Mary *are living in Nazareth*, then go to Bethlehem, where they find no room in the inn. Forty days later Jesus is taken to the temple, and the family returns to its home in Nazareth. There are no Wise Men, and Jesus was back in Nazareth long before the Magi would have arrived. For Matthew, Joseph and Mary *are living in Bethlehem*, no shepherds greet them at the time of Jesus' birth, and they are still in their Bethlehem home (not in an inn) where the Magi find them a year or two later. The family then flees to Egypt for a time; and for fear of Herod, they do not return to their home in Bethlehem, but take up a *new* residence in Nazareth. The two stories cannot be reconciled.

## Why the Evangelists Could Have Created Their Stories

One defense of the Nativity narratives has been to say that they were never intended to be histories, but rather to proclaim religious or

*False Questions*

theological truths. Still, one wonders why the evangelists created these stories. Here are some possibilities:

*First*, it was common knowledge that Jesus grew up in Nazareth in Galilee. That Jesus' roots were widely known is obvious from the sign that Pilate placed on Jesus' cross, which read, "Jesus of Nazareth, king of the Jews."

*Next*, every Jew knew that Galileans could not trace their ancestry to David or Abraham.

*Third*, we have to be aware of what the evangelists *believed* to be true. For Matthew, Jesus was the *Jewish Messiah*. For Luke, Jesus was the Messiah, but the promised prophet as well, both for Jews *and Gentiles*, as is evident from the Acts of the Apostles.

If Jesus was the Messiah, then he must have fulfilled the Hebrew Scriptures, which taught that the Messiah would be a son of David and born in Bethlehem:

> [40] When the people heard [Jesus], some said, "This is indeed the prophet." [41] Others said, "He is the Messiah." Still others said, "The, Messiah cannot come from Galilee, can he? [42] Doesn't the scripture say that the Messiah will come from the house of David and from Bethlehem, David's village?" [43] And so the crowd was divided about Jesus. [44] Some wanted to arrest him, but no one laid hands on him.[35]

The evangelists faced two dilemmas. If Jesus was of Galilean ancestry, he could not at the same time be descended from David. And if he grew up in Nazareth, why would his parents be in Bethlehem for his birth?

## The Genealogies

Each evangelist solved the problem of Jesus' ancestry by producing a genealogy. Matthew's genealogy, in going back to Abraham, showed that Jesus was primarily the *Jewish* Messiah. The genealogy for Luke, going

---

35  John 7:40-44

back to Adam, was in line with his intention of showing that Jesus was the prophet sent to save *both Jews and Gentiles*. Because of their distinct theological intentions, minor differences in the genealogies should not be surprising. Ordinarily we presume the validity of genealogies, since every family would know its ancestry and had to be able to prove it. Most people have no difficulty in giving the names of their parents and grandparents, and some can go back many generations. If Joseph had been a descendant of Abraham and David, he could have documented it; and Jesus, James and the rest of his family could have done so as well.

We do not know the sources Luke and Matthew used to construct their genealogies. To be authentic, the family of Joseph and Mary would have to be the original source of their information. Consequently, most of the names in the immediate ancestry ought to be identical or nearly so. And yet, the names between David and Joseph are *all* different, with Luke tracing Joseph's genealogy back to David through Nathan, and Matthew through Solomon. We could overlook discrepancies beyond seven or eight generations, but how can we explain discrepancies in naming Joseph's father and grandfather? Matthew names Jacob, Matthan and Eleazar as the father, grandfather and great-grandfather of Joseph, whereas Luke lists Heli, Matthat and Levi respectively. Who was Joseph's father? Was it Jacob or Heli? Matthew and Luke cannot both be right.

Early Christian writers were aware of these discrepancies, and they usually solved the problem by choosing one genealogy over the other, reasoning, I suppose, that one of them had to be correct. But we have no data to affirm that either Matthew or Luke used reliable testimony. One or both were either given false information or made up their ancestral list. If we try to think as the evangelists thought, then perhaps they assumed that if Jesus was the Messiah, then he *had* to be a son of David, and it made little difference whether their genealogies listed any of Joseph's actual ancestors.

The evangelists would have thought that since Jesus was the Messiah, he must have been born in Bethlehem. They created stories, each with quasi-historical details, such as an empire-wide census or the slaughter of children, in order to fulfill a prophecy about the Messiah's birth in

*False Questions*

Jerusalem and at the same time keep intact the acknowledged fact that Jesus was a Galilean who grew up in Nazareth.

## Matthew's Prophecies

Matthew's way of thinking becomes clear by examining how he used the Old Testament. "Out of Egypt I have called my son" comes from Hosea,[36] and it refers to God's delivery of the Israelites from slavery in Egypt. It has no relevance to Jesus' return from Egypt. In reference to the massacre of the children by Herod, he quotes Jeremiah: "Rachel bewailing her children."[37] There is nothing in the quotation to connect it with Herod's supposed atrocity. He tells us that Joseph settled in Nazareth so that "what was said through the prophets would be fulfilled: 'He shall be called a Nazorean.'"[38] No one knows where Matthew got that quotation. Did Matthew find prophecies that confirmed his story, or did he make his story fit the predictions?

Since most of the infancy narratives lack historical foundation, what are we to make of the central event, the virgin birth? Matthew supports this event with another Old Testament prophecy, "The virgin shall be with child,"[39] Again he changes the meaning of the prophet's words. The word he quotes as "virgin" actually means "maiden" or young woman in the original Hebrew, and Isaiah refers to the birth of a child in his immediate future. This is another case of a misinterpreted prophecy.[40]

## Luke's Leitmotif

Luke says that Jesus was "as was thought" or "as was supposed"[41] the son of Joseph. This implies that there was no suspicion that Joseph was not the father of Jesus; therefore he was not writing to defend against

---

36  Hosea 11:1
37  Jeremiah 31:15
38  Matthew 2:23
39  Isaiah 7:14
40  A detailed analysis of Isaiah 7:10-17 is found in Appendix C.
41  Luke 3:23

rumors that Jesus was illegitimate. Instead, Luke's purpose in narrating the virgin birth is found in what modern scholars call a leitmotif.

Hebrew writers and story tellers often used a leitmotif, which is a story template. One frequently used is that of a man meeting a woman at a well. Those who were listening to these stories knew what was almost always going to happen: the man would meet his future bride. This leitmotif is found in Genesis 24, where Abraham's servant finds a bride for Isaac at a well; in Genesis 29, where Jacob meets Rachel at a well; and in Exodus 2, where Moses meets the seven daughters of a Midianite priest at a well, and one is given to him in marriage. The story of Jesus and the Samaritan woman in John 4 may be a reflection of this leitmotif.

Luke uses the Old Testament leitmotif of a miraculous birth of a male child. For example, in Genesis 21Sarah bore a son for Abraham when she was past child-bearing age. In Genesis 29 Leah, Jacob's wife, was unable to bear children. God saw that she was unloved by Jacob, so God "opened her womb" and she bore four sons, the youngest of whom was Judah, the ancestor of David. In Judges 13 we have a similar story about the birth of Samson. And in First Samuel 1, Hannah, the wife of Eli, prays to God and gives birth to the prophet Samuel. Some characteristics of this story pattern are the annunciation of the birth by a heavenly messenger and the naming of the child either by God or by the mother instead of the father, as in the births of Samson and Samuel.

In the leitmotif of the miraculous birth, God intervenes so that the mother can conceive a male child, who turns out to be a hero or an unusually important person. The name of the child can also have special significance.

Luke uses this template first for the birth of John the Baptist. Zechariah and Elizabeth had no children, and both were elderly. An angel announced to Zechariah that his wife would bear a child, and, as with Abraham, told what to name him. Like Samuel, John became a famous prophet.

An added detail in the story of John the Baptist is that when Mary greets Elizabeth, John leaped for joy while in his mother's womb. This is to tell us that John, even before birth, recognized that Jesus was greater than he.

Since Jesus is supposed to be superior to John, then his birth should be more miraculous than John's. Hence there is a second miraculous story, a virgin birth. In all the other stories of this genre, the mother was either past childbearing age or for some other reason unable to have children. This would not work with Mary. The need for a "super" miracle can explain why Luke put a virgin birth into his narrative, at least from a literary and theological perspective.

## Summary

In conclusion, the infancy narratives are theological statements and/or literary devices expressing the belief that Jesus was preordained to be the Messiah and Israel's greatest prophet. The evangelists seem to relate Old Testament predictions that fit the life of Jesus, when in reality the details of Jesus birth and ancestry are contrived and lack historical foundation. The virgin birth, as a miracle story, can never be proved. Neither can it be supported as the fulfillment of Isaiah 7:14; those who accept it do so as a matter of personal faith.

## B. Jesus as the Suffering Servant

Matthew and Luke sought to show how Jesus fulfilled the scriptures in their infancy narratives. Mark makes the same effort in the way he relates the passion.

### Mark's Use of Psalm 22 as an Outline for the Passion

The key to Mark's passion story is Psalm 22, since the words that Jesus spoke, "Eloi, Eloi, lema sabachtani?" (meaning, "My God, my God, why have you forsaken me?") are the beginning of the psalm. This prayer reveals Mark's whole theological argument. Psalm 22 proceeds to speak of suffering on the part of the speaker, but turns to deliverance both for the one praying and for the people, and concludes by looking forward to a glorious future. Mark modeled his passion narrative on this psalm, showing that Jesus was not the messiah in spite of his suffering, but *because* of it.

Chapter 15 of Mark has a number of obvious parallels in Psalm 22: Verses 17, 20 and 31-32 express the theme of mocking found in Psalm 22:6-7. Dividing the clothes and casting lots for them is found in Mark 15:24 and Psalm 22:18. Psalm 22:15 has the speaker's mouth dried up, and in Mark 15:23 Jesus is given wine mixed with myrrh to drink.

### The Contrast between the Passion in Mark and Luke

Mark's account of the passion is not a historical narrative, but a theological argument constructing the story on an outline of Psalm 22. The freedom the evangelists had in creating their narratives can be illustrated by comparing the passion found in Mark with that of Luke. Jesus in Mark prays three times for God to take the cup of suffering from him and from the cross asks, "My God, my God, why have you forsaken me?"[42] In Luke Jesus in the Mount of Olives petitions God only once, while adding "but your will be done."[43] And in the passion he is in total control, telling

---

42  Mark 15:34
43  Luke 22:39-46

the women along the way, "Don't weep for me, but for yourselves and your children,"[44] and calmly reassuring the repentant criminal, "today you will be with me in paradise."[45] Jesus even asks God to forgive those responsible for his death — "Father, forgive them, for they don't know what they are doing"[46] — and dies with these words on his lips, "Father, into your hands I commend my spirit."[47] The passion story in Mark is not the same passion story as found in Luke. The two narratives do not even describe the same Jesus.

Mark makes no explicit claim that Jesus fulfilled Psalm 22 by his suffering. Instead, he composed his story in a way to make it fit the psalm. Versions of the other evangelists are markedly different, so much so that few refer to Psalm 22 as a prediction about the messiah.

## The Suffering Servant of Isaiah

Far different is the theme of the Suffering Servant found in Isaiah 53, which is the subject of countless disputes. Some argue from a strictly theological or dogmatic point of view, pointing out that details found in Isaiah 53 are a good match for the life of Jesus. These arguments are not convincing. There are rules on how to interpret sacred Scripture, and they begin with an analysis of the vocabulary, intention and context, both literary and historical, of the author. We can also consider how others closer in time to the biblical text understood the author. There are numerous analyses of Isaiah 53, and I suggest giving special attention to how Jewish scholars interpret Isaiah, which is, after all, a part of Jewish scripture.

The central question in Isaiah 53 is whether the author is talking about the future messiah or the nation of Israel. Often overlooked is the context of the book of Isaiah, which actually has *four* separate Suffering

---

44   Luke 23:26-31
45   Luke 23:43. Some translators capitalize "paradise," but it is not capitalized in the Greek version.
46   Luke 23:34
47   Luke 23:46

Servant Songs: Isaiah 42:1-4, 49:1-6, 50:4-9 and 52:13-53:12. In Isaiah 49:3 the servant is explicitly identified with the nation. References to Israel in the masculine singular as God's servant are found throughout Isaiah, but sometimes we know that the author is identifying the servant as Israel from the occasional use of the plural, as in Isaiah 52:3. Also significant is that the sufferings of the servant are in the *past* tense, while the servant's glorification is placed in the *future*.

We have to agree with those Jewish scholars who assert that the servant described in Isaiah is the nation of Israel and *only* the nation of Israel.

The disciples were convinced that Jesus was the Messiah, and that there had to be proof of this in the Old Testament. They certainly tried hard to find it — sometimes too hard, and they molded their stories to fit their "prophecies" rather than finding a legitimate prediction.

## Our Answer

Our question for this chapter was, *how can we prove that Jesus was the promised Jewish Messiah?* Appealing to Old Testament prophecies does not work. This question, like the others before it, is based on the fallacy that Jesus fulfilled what was predicted. The Jews of his time expected someone altogether different, a glorious conqueror who would liberate Israel from Rome. If he had fulfilled these expectations, he would have been readily accepted.

Our answer, then, is that *we cannot prove that Jesus was the promised Messiah*. This belief is based entirely on his being raised from the dead. There is no proof for the resurrection, and it can be accepted only as religious doctrine or faith.

CHAPTER 4

# The Passion

We have discussed the theological problem of why Jesus was crucified. In this chapter I will address the historical reasons for his execution, insofar as we can determine from the Gospels.

There are two parts to this topic: 1) the decision to kill Jesus, and 2) the charges brought against him.

# A. The Plot to Kill Jesus

After teaching in Galilee, Jesus went to Jerusalem to celebrate the Passover. The week started off well with a celebratory entry into the city, but suddenly, within a week, he was arrested, sentenced and crucified.

In Luke 23:5 his accusers alleged that "he stirs up the people by teaching…" The expressed concern is about public disruption, but disruption caused by his *teaching*. All the charges against Jesus relate to *what he taught*. Our question, then, for this section is, *what did Jesus teach that made those in power decide to kill him?*

## The Cleansing of the Temple

The turning point from triumphal entry to crucifixion is, I believe, found in an episode called the "Cleansing of the Temple." The event is recorded in all four Gospels:

> **Mark**
> [15]They then came to Jerusalem. And [Jesus] entered the temple and began to drive out those who were selling and buying there, and he turned over the tables of the money exchangers and the seats of those selling doves; [16]and he kept anyone from carrying anything through the temple. [17]He taught them with these words, "Isn't it written, 'My house will be called a house of prayer for all nations?' But you have made it a robbers' den." [18]And when the chief priests and the scribes heard of this, they began to look for a way to kill him; they were afraid of him, because all the people were entranced by his teaching. [19]And in the evening, Jesus and his disciples left the city.[48]
>
> **Matthew**
> [12]Then Jesus went into the temple and drove out all those who were buying and selling in the temple, and turned over the tables of the money exchangers and the seats of those selling doves. [13]He said to them, "It is written, 'My house will be called a house

---

48  Mark 11:15-19

of prayer" but you have made it a robbers' den.'" ¹⁴Then the blind and the lame approached him in the temple, and he healed them.

¹⁵But when the chief priests and scribes saw the incredible things that he did, and the children crying out in the temple, saying, "Hosanna to the son of David!" they were furious ¹⁶and said to him, "Do you hear what they are saying?"

And Jesus said to them, "Yes. Have you never read, 'You have brought perfect praise out of the mouth of babies and infants?'"[49]

## Luke

⁴⁵Then [Jesus] entered the temple and began to drive out of there those who were selling; ⁴⁶he said, "It is written, 'My house will be a house of prayer'; but you have made it a robber's den." ⁴⁷Each day he taught in the temple. The chief priests, the scribes, and the leaders of the people began to look for a way to kill him; ⁴⁸but they were at a loss, for all the people were entranced by what they heard.[50]

## John

¹³It was near the time of the Passover of the Jews, and Jesus went up to Jerusalem. ¹⁴In the temple he found those who were selling cattle, sheep, and doves, along with the money exchangers sitting at their tables. ¹⁵He made a whip from some cords, and then he drove them all out of the temple, along with their sheep and the cattle. And he scattered the coins of the money exchangers and turned over their tables. ¹⁶He said to those selling doves, "Get rid of these things! Don't make my Father's house a market!" ¹⁷His disciples remembered the writing, "Zeal for your house will engulf me."

¹⁸The Jews replied to him, "What sign can you do for us to justify this?"

¹⁹Jesus answered, "Destroy this temple, and in three days I will raise it up."

---

49  Matthew 21:12-16
50  Luke 19:45-48

> ²⁰The Jews then said, "They have been building this temple for forty-six years, and you are going to raise it up in three days?"²¹But he was speaking of the temple of his body. ²²After he had been raised from the dead, his disciples remembered what he had said; and they believed the scripture and the word Jesus had said.[51]

Mark is the earliest Gospel, from which Luke and Matthew copied. In some cases Luke and Matthew use common material not found in Mark. This is called "Q," which stands for the German word for source. In this story we find no common new details in Matthew and Luke which are not found in Mark. Instead of adding details, these two evangelists have each shortened the story. Since Mark was writing before the other two, who simply revised Mark's story, the version of the cleansing in Mark is preferred over Luke and Matthew.

It is possible that John had access to a version of this story older than Mark's, even though John was written a generation later; but the only added detail is that Jesus made a whip of cords. This could come from a very early account, or it could be added through years of retelling the story. In either case, John offers no new significant information.

### John's Version of the Cleansing

John's version differs by placing the story at the beginning of Jesus' ministry rather than at the end. The common opinion is that John and the Synoptic evangelists (Mark, Matthew and Luke) all relate the same event. Why would John make this modification?

John's placement of the Cleansing of the Temple could have theological reasons behind it. This Gospel stresses the belief that Jesus consistently worked miracles or "signs" as proof of his mission and divinity. We see this theology here. The cleansing leads the Jews to ask Jesus, "What sign can you show us for doing this?" This in turn enables John to turn the conversation into Jesus' prediction of his most significant sign, his resurrection. Throughout his Gospel, John expresses little concern for what

---

51  John 2:13-22

Jesus does, except for signs that prove who Jesus is. John seems to have placed the Cleansing of the Temple at the beginning of Jesus' ministry so that Jesus could predict a sign to take place at the very end of the Gospel.

For several reasons, then, Mark's version seems preferable to John's: 1) John adds no significant details. 2) John's placement and use of the story appears to be determined by a theological motive. 3) There is no evidence that John had access to a version of the story earlier than Mark's.

The Cleansing of the Temple is found in two *independent* sources, Mark and John, making historical roots for the story likely. Mark's version, since written earlier, is probably based on earlier historical data. Our analysis of this event, then, is based on Mark.

## Differences Among the Synoptic Gospels

There are several significant differences among the Synoptic Gospels. Although all three record Jesus as quoting Isaiah 56:7 as the reason for his actions: "My house shall be called a house of prayer for all the nations," Luke and Matthew shorten this quotation. We can speculate that their reason for dropping "for all the nations" may be that they preferred to emphasize Jesus as the *Jewish* prophet. This is my personal speculation.

Luke places the Cleansing of the Temple after the description of Jesus weeping over Jerusalem, regretting its future destruction. Since he was writing after the destruction of the temple, he may have seen the story of the cleansing as a fuller illustration of Jesus' love for the temple and the holy city.

Matthew places the story immediately after Jesus triumphantly enters Jerusalem, with the crowd shouting, "Hosanna to the son of David." He ends the story of the cleansing with the children in the temple crying out with the same refrain. For Matthew, then, the cleansing is the conclusion of the story of Jesus' entry into Jerusalem.

For Mark, on the other hand, the Cleansing of the Temple is a turning point in his Gospel. Everything for Jesus had been going smoothly through his triumphal entry into Jerusalem. But right after the cleansing, the chief priests and the scribes were looking for a way to kill him.

## Proposed Reasons for the Decision to Kill Jesus

A number of reasons have been proposed to explain why Jesus' actions made the chief priests and elders determined to kill him. One theory suggests that Jesus opposed the temple itself, since he predicted its destruction. Besides the predictions found in the Synoptic Gospels, there is also the prediction recorded in the fourth chapter of John, when Jesus speaks to the Samaritan woman at the well. The woman asserts that God was to be worshiped on Mt. Gerizim, and Jesus replies that the hour was coming when the Father would be worshiped neither on Mt. Gerizim nor in Jerusalem. He says that God is spirit, and all are to worship God in spirit and in truth.

However, he wept over Jerusalem,[52] and the words he quoted from Isaiah 56:7 in our passage from Mark 11 indicate a defense of the temple — even an extension of its spiritual domain to "all the nations" — rather than opposition.

The Gospels relate that Jesus predicted the destruction of the temple, but nowhere, including the story of the cleansing, do they imply that he wanted it to happen.

John's version, since it was written long after the destruction of the temple, is more a reflection of his theological viewpoint than of the attitude of Jesus, and does not contradict Mark 11 or Luke 19.

A similar hypothesis is that Jesus wanted to do away with temple sacrifices, but this cannot be reconciled with his celebration of Passover. All Passover lambs had to be slain in the temple. If a layman assisted in this, a priest had to collect the blood and ritually dispose of it. The Passover lambs had to be eaten in the city of Jerusalem. That the Jews considered the slaughter of the Passover lambs a true sacrifice is absolutely certain.[53] If Jesus celebrated the Passover meal, then he participated in temple sacrifice.

---

52 Luke 19:41-44
53 Jeremias, Joachim, *Jerusalem in the Time of Jesus,* Fortress Press, Philadelphia, 1969, page 78.

If Jesus had pronounced the end of temple sacrifices, then the apostles would have refused to participate in them. In Acts the apostles continued to live as faithful Jews, worshiping in the temple:

> [46]Each day they spent time together in the temple. They broke bread in their homes and ate their food with joy and generosity, [47]praising God and enjoying the goodwill of all the people. And every day the Lord increased the number of those who were being saved.[54]

Also in Acts James advises Paul to participate in temple sacrifice:

> [26]Then Paul took the men, and the next day, after purifying himself, he went into the temple with them, showing publicly that the days of purification, during which a sacrifice would be offered for each one, were completed.[55]

Paul's going to the temple for sacrifice was under the approval and advice of "James and all the elders."[56] James, the head of the Jerusalem church and brother of Jesus, remained a practicing Jew and asked Paul to have the temple sacrifice made for Paul and his four companions.

Finally, for Jesus to pronounce the end of the temple sacrifices would be the only time in the Gospels when he would have signaled the least opposition to Judaic laws or customs.

## The Temple Complex

Mark's account of the cleansing must be put it into its historical context:

Although Herod's temple was destroyed by the Romans in 70 C.E., we have enough detailed descriptions and measurements from ancient literature that reasonably accurate depictions and models have been

---

54   Acts 2:46-47
55   Acts 21:26
56   Acts 21:17-26

made. The whole structure, called the Temple Mount, stood thirty meters or ten stories high. The top floor was an immense plaza in trapezoidal shape, measuring approximately 533 yards on the western wall, 503 on the eastern, 345 on the northern and 306 on the southern. The area was over 172,000 square yards, big enough to hold twenty American football fields and 100,000 people.

Off center, running from east to west, with more open space on the south, was the main temple complex or building, which only Jews could enter. The Holy of Holies was at the west end of the building, and at the east was the entrance, leading first to the Court of the Women, then to other areas for men, Levites and priests. The entire open area outside the temple building was the Court of the Gentiles.

Most scholars place the Cleansing of the Temple in the mammoth Court of the Gentiles. The rooms inside the temple building were too small to house any significant number of businesses or tables for money changers.

Mark says that Jesus "would not allow anyone to carry anything through the temple." How he could accomplish this is puzzling. The Court of the Gentiles is so vast that no one person could have covered the entire area or guarded both sides of the temple structure at the same time. Nor could he have blocked all the gates into the temple building. To keep people from entering the Court of the Gentiles, he would have had to block four gates on the north and two on the south. Maybe he was aided by his followers.

## Reasons for Jesus' Actions

The other actions of Jesus make sense. He drove out those who were buying and selling, and he overturned the tables of the money changers. All this took place in the Court of the Gentiles and not in the temple building, which only Jews could enter. This leads to the following questions:

First, *should Jesus' actions be interpreted symbolically, as a desire to destroy the temple?* No, since his words indicate no such desire, nor is there any other past or future event that the cleansing could symbolize.

Some say that the cleansing was an acted-out parable, but the Gospels give no indication of this, nor do we find any Gospel stories of Jesus acting out his parables or other messages. The closest thing we have is when Jesus curses the fig tree.[57]

Second, since the Cleansing of the Temple took place in the Court of the Gentiles, *was Jesus demanding that the entire Temple Mount should be kept holy, and not just the temple building?* Yes seems to be the appropriate answer, since Jesus was teaching that the temple should be "a house of prayer for all the nations." However, it is unlikely that Jesus would have demanded that *all* businesses be banned from the plaza or Court of the Gentiles area. The Temple Mount was built with the plaza area, especially around the perimeter, to be a place for markets and businesses. It would have been similar in use to a Roman forum. The businesses that were the most likely to arouse Jesus' anger would have been those selling animals, especially since the prices were exorbitantly inflated, and the money changers. And these are the businesses explicitly named in the Gospels.

Third, *was the disturbance in the temple the main reason for the anger of the chief priests?* Any serious disturbance in or outside the temple could result in Roman armed intervention. Fear of this may have been a motivating factor, but the Gospel points to other factors as well. Above all, there is no hint that Jesus was rebelling against Rome or had any intention to do so. Roman soldiers were in a tower, overlooking the Temple Mount, especially on religious holidays such as Passover, and the Gospels omit any mention of Roman concern or intervention at the time of this event.

## Jesus and the Merchants

Fourth, *why did Jesus protest businesses in the temple?* There would have been many commercial groups or markets in the huge expanse surrounding the temple, but the ones Jesus protested were, besides the

---

57  Matthew 21:18-22

money changers, those selling animals for sacrifice. Pilgrims usually found it difficult to bring any animals from afar, and if an animal had a blemish of any kind, it would have been rejected. Therefore, visitors to Jerusalem found it convenient, if not necessary, to buy their sacrificial animals at the temple. What was unconscionable was that these animals were often sold at many, many times their value.

### Jesus and the Money Changers

Fifth, *why did Jesus protest the money changers in the temple?* The money changers were actually carrying out an essential function for the temple. It was their job to collect the temple tax, which was to be paid once a year by every adult male. They began their work each year in various locations throughout the country, and set up tables in the temple only a short time before Passover. In the temple they collected the tax from those who had not yet paid and changed foreign money into the coinage required for any temple offering. This exchange of currency enabled pilgrims from other territories to exchange their coins for the acceptable coinage.

The requirement for a specific kind of coin necessitated money changers. The only coin acceptable was minted in Tyre and called the Tyrian tetradrachma, or sometimes the Tyrian shekel or silver shekel. The Tyrian coin was chosen because of its purity, being close to ninety-five percent pure silver. It was stamped with the figure of a pagan god (Heracles/Hercules), which should have made it unacceptable; but the temple authorities judged the coin's purity to be more important.

### The Temple Tax

The tax for adult males was a half shekel. To make sure that at least the half shekel was paid, the tax collectors (or money changers) charged a small extra payment, part of which was to pay them for their work.

Tetradrachma literally means four drachmas. Since one drachma seems to have been a day's wages for a Roman soldier or for a worker in a vineyard, half a Tyrian tetradrachma has been equated with wages for two days.

This equivalency is not the whole picture. A Roman soldier may have received a drachma every day, but Jewish peasants had no guarantee of being employed every day. This was especially true of farmers and peasants, such as those in Galilee and other territories outside Judea, who found it difficult to come up with a half Tyrian tetradrachma. Besides, the coin was not used in daily commerce by the Jews, who had to go to a money changer to purchase one either for the temple tax or for an animal sacrifice. The need for a Tyrian coin was an added hardship for the many Jews living on the edge.

The ancient law requiring a tax to be paid to the temple specified that it be paid only *once in a lifetime*, when an adult male reached the age of twenty. By the first century, sometime after the Maccabean revolt, the law had been expanded to demand payment *annually* after the age of twenty. This was another reason why the poor found the law a burden and Jesus would become angry.

Jesus himself was one of the poor. He (and/or his father Joseph) is described in Greek as a *tektōn*,[58] universally translated as carpenter, but whose actual meaning is more likely a laborer or someone who works with his hands. The traditional translation as carpenter is out of place, because of the lack of wood to work with in Nazareth. But *tektōn* certainly does not mean an artisan or skilled workman. Jesus came from Nazareth in Galilee, and he preached mainly to Galileans. There was no middle class there. Most were poor, living just a little above the subsistence level. Jesus was one of these, and he identified with them.

## Follow the Money

Sixth, *who were the responsible parties for the evils Jesus was protesting?* If the businesses and money changers were acting entirely on their own, then we would expect the chief priests and elders to say something like, "We regret what was going on. We were unaware of what these people were doing, but we will make sure it no longer happens." Instead,

---

58  Matthew 13:55, Mark 6:3

they questioned Jesus, "By what authority are you doing these things?"[59] By defending their authority, they admitted that they had allowed the businesses and money changers to operate in the temple. The primary ones to blame, then, were not the merchants and money changers, but the chief priests and elders.

Seventh, *who were profiting from the money made in the temple?* We need to "follow the money." The temple, of course, had expenses to meet, but in contrast to the poor and the common people in Israel, there was an aristocratic class that had wealth beyond the dreams of anyone else. These were the temple priests.

When Jerusalem was destroyed in 70 C.E., it was unlivable and most had either deserted or been killed. But through archeological research in the city we have learned much about the lives of the temple priests. Their homes were prime real estate, located on a hill west of the temple, with a sublime vista of the temple and the city, and enjoying a cool breeze during most of the year.

Excavations of the homes in the Jewish quarter reveal much about the inhabitants' lifestyle. The houses had marble panels and frescoes, beautiful mosaic floors, and were decorated in the latest Roman styles, except that there were no figured images because of religious prohibitions. The homes were also distinguished by the numerous Jewish ritual baths.

The elite enjoyed an expensive Second Pompeian type of decorations and living quarters, including the best imported dinner ware and stone furniture. One singular find was a broken vase by Ennion, a renowned glass blower in Phoenicia, north of Israel. Among the archeological finds are examples of the best imported glassware and dishes.

In one of the homes excavated in the Jewish quarter the words "Bar Kathros" were found inscribed in stone. Since Kathros was the name of a priestly family, we know for certain that the priests lived among the very wealthy in the Jewish quarter. The temple priests, together with the

---

59   Mark 11:27

Sadducees, comprised a social class with a life of luxury on a par with the richest in the Roman Empire. All of this was supported under the auspices of religion.

## The High Priesthood

Eighth, *Jesus may have objected to the Jewish high priesthood as illegitimate.* When Solomon built the first Temple, he appointed Zadok as high priest, and his descendants continued in that office until the Maccabean revolt in the second century B.C.E. Under the Maccabeans (or Hasmoneans), the Zadokites lost control of the high priesthood, and the family broke into three branches, while the high priest was appointed by the king or ruler and eventually by Rome.

One branch of the Zadokites left Israel and established another temple in Leontopolis in Egypt. This was closed by Vespasian in 73 C.E.

Another Zadokite group established and led the community at Qumran.

A third group of the family of Zadok stayed in Jerusalem. They went along with whoever was in power, whether Jew or Gentile. By the late first century B.C.E., they had become part of the Jewish elite and were known as the Sadducees. Later on the term "Sadducee" (derived from the name of Zadok) could include anyone of the Jewish upper class, and as such, they were politically conservative. They were also religiously conservative, refusing to believe in life after death because it was not written in the Torah. They believed in total free will, independent of God, and therefore denied God's foreknowledge.

Joining the Sadducees in the wealthy class were the priests of Jerusalem. In recent times archeologists discovered an ossuary, or stone box for the bones of the deceased, with the name of Caiaphas inscribed on it. This has been accepted as the burial box of Caiaphas, the high priest at the time of Jesus, and of his family. Only the very rich had ossuaries, and this ossuary shows that Caiaphas was one of them.

As a result, Jesus may have objected to the temple priests as illegitimate, since they were not of the line of Zadok, and he disagreed with the Sadducees concerning life after death.

The last verses of the cleansing story in Mark tell us that the chief priests and scribes "were afraid of [Jesus], because all the people were entranced by his teaching."[60] Mark makes it clear that these leaders were concerned about Jesus' teachings, but because it made him appealing to the people, and not necessarily because they disagreed with what he taught. Instead, the chief priests made their decision to kill Jesus because he took action against those who had made the temple into a robber's den.

In conclusion, various reasons have been proposed for why Jesus was executed. Some think that the message of the kingdom of God assumed that Jesus himself was a king, but Jesus never taught that he was a king. I will address this further in the next section.

The worst concoction to explain the crucifixion is to blame it on the Jewish people or nation. We find the roots of this anti-Jewish sentiment already in the Gospel of John.

Mark explains why Jesus' ministry turned from a celebratory welcome into Jerusalem into a decision to put him to death. He exposed the evils going on in the name of religion. He challenged those responsible. He pitted himself directly against the wealthy and powerful, and he took the side of the poor and oppressed. He defended the temple as a loyal and faithful Jew, and protested its being used to oppress his people. Those in power saw the murder of Jesus as the only way to eliminate the threat to curtail their cash flow and luxurious life style.

Jesus was crucified because he defended the poor and oppressed.

## Our Answer

Our question for this section was, *what did Jesus teach that made those in power decide to kill him?* Again, there is a fallacious assumption behind this question. Those in power made their decision not because of what he taught, but *because he was a threat to their wealthy life style, supported by defrauding the people.*

---

60  Mark 11:18

## B. The Death Sentence

Jesus' disciples searched for a reason why their Messiah had to suffer and die. Gentile converts looked for someone to blame for his execution. Since the Gospels and other early writings were written mostly for Gentile believers, they avoided finding fault with the imperial government, instead blaming the Jews. The Epistle of Barnabas, written between 70 and 135 C.E. (not authored by the Barnabas who accompanied the apostle Paul), was vehement in its hatred of the Jews, and is listed among the writings of the apostolic fathers. Fortunately, it never made it into the New Testament canon.

Today most Christians understand that regardless of the role of Jewish leaders in condemning Jesus, the Jewish people bear no responsibility for his death. Since Pontius Pilate, Rome's man in charge, alone sentenced Jesus, legal responsibility falls on Pilate and Rome.

In the previous section I explored the reason why the Jewish leaders decided to have Jesus put to death. Our question now is, *what were Pilate's legal charges against Jesus?*

The passion narratives are our only sources directly relating to Jesus' trial. All accounts are primarily theological, with any historical data modified to support their theological perspective.

### The Theory of Peasant Rebels

The abrupt change from the public ministry to the tragedy of the passion is heightened by the unexpected accusations against Jesus. The charges include claiming to be the messiah, the son of man, the son of God and king of the Jews. These titles do appear occasionally in the Gospels, but the major charge of claiming to be king of the Jews is not found in the Gospels except in the passion narratives. In Matthew 2:2 the wise men look for "the child born king of the Jews" and in John 12:13 the crowds hail Jesus as the "king of Israel" as he enters the holy city. Otherwise the title of king appears only as questions from Pilate.

Pilate put the sign "Jesus of Nazareth, king of the Jews" above Jesus' crucifix, and this charge could have come only from those who turned

Jesus in. What was actually said between Jesus and Pilate is not known, since the disciples had no access to Pilate's chambers during the trial. The evangelists could only have constructed these conversations from rumors that were circulating. They could also have made up some details for theological or other reasons.

Scholars have advanced various theories about why Jesus was put to death. One is that he was causing disturbances that worried the Jewish and/or the Roman authorities. We have no evidence that Rome was focused on his activities, and the Gospels do not mention any disturbances.

Some assert that Jesus and his band of apostles were peasant rebels. They claim that there is a hint of this when Simon is called "the Zealot."[61] They ask why any of his followers would be carrying swords, because when Jesus is arrested one of his followers draws his sword and cuts off someone's ear. As time went on this follower was identified as Simon Peter in John 18:10. This argument fails to acknowledge that Jesus reproved the swordsman and never advocated violence. It also shows an ignorance of how nicknames are used. For example, if we enter a German restaurant employing twelve Germans and one Korean, and then ask for the Korean, the manager will know at once the one we want to see. But to ask for the German will leave the manager confused. Nor will the manager know whom we seek if we ask for the Korean when there are two Koreans employed. Nicknames make no sense if they apply to more than one person in a group. To call Simon the Zealot, tells us that he is the *only one* of the apostles to whom that description applies.

## The Charge of Insurrection

One reason to think of Jesus and his apostles as rebels is that the Gospels absolve Pilate and blame the Jews for the crucifixion. Pilate is pictured as wanting to release Jesus while the Jews cry out for his death. Since it is scarcely believable that the Jewish populace demanded Jesus'

---

61  Luke 6:15; Acts 1:13

*False Questions*

execution, we have to look for another reason for Pilate's decision to go ahead with it. That reason would be insurrection.

Of course, almost any infraction of Roman law would work. The charges that do not work would be breaking Jewish law, such as by blasphemy. This is what the high priest accused Jesus of,[62] but it was not what the chief priests charged him with when they handed him over;[63] the accusations included perverting the nation and forbidding the payment of taxes to Rome, but also claiming to be messiah and king.

To say that Pilate must have used insurrection as his reason for condemning Jesus has no foundation in Jesus' activities as told in the Gospels, which are the only sources of information that we have.

## The Theories of Secret Teaching and No Burial

Some modern authors rewrite the story of Jesus' passion and death. Here is a composite of what some propose really happened in place of what the Gospels relate:

> *We start with the betrayal. When Judas went to the chief priests, they must have wanted something worth their money, and that turned out to be a secret teaching of Jesus to be used against him. Since all evangelists report that Pilate questioned Jesus on a single topic, "Are you the king of the Jews?" the secret teaching passed on from Judas to the priests and then to Pilate was that Jesus claimed to be king of the Jews.*
>
> *Therefore, the theory goes, Pilate condemned Jesus because of this secret teaching, a claim equivalent to insurrection against Rome. Jesus was then crucified as a revolutionary, which is what Rome did to all who created disturbances by claiming to be a messiah. Since Roman sol-*

---

62  Matthew 26:65; Mark 14:64
63  Luke 23:1-2

*diers always left bodies on their crosses until they decayed, and then put them in a common grave, this is what must have happened to Jesus; there is no possibility that the release of Jesus' body would have been an exception.*

In answering the question about Pilate's legal charges, I will also respond to these recently proposed ideas about Jesus' passion and death. I will disregard details that are clearly theological in nature and that may manipulate historical details. For example, when Mark uses Psalm 22 as an outline of his story, we question whether his details are historical facts. Since there is no historical evidence of a custom of releasing a prisoner on Passover, we question the historicity of this detail. And since Barabbas literally means "son of the father," the choice between "Jesus, king of the Jews" and "Jesus, son of the father" sounds like a theological creation, even though it is hard to decipher. The story of the dream of Pilate's wife is also unlikely to be historical.

The theory of a secret teaching interprets the betrayal in a way that conflicts with the Gospel stories, which presume that the betrayal occurs when Judas kisses his master and not when he is paid. Only *after* being paid did he *look for* an opportunity to betray him.[64] At the last supper Jesus says that "one of you will betray me,"[65] indicating that the betrayal had not yet happened. In the garden Jesus asks Judas, "Are you betraying the son of man with a kiss?"[66] In this case the betrayal is happening in the here and now, not sometime in the past. This theory implies that the evangelists either did not know the facts or deliberately hid what happened.

## The Charge of Being King of the Jews

Since Pilate asked Jesus if he was king of the Jews, we ask whether Jesus ever made that assertion. If so, he would have to have been a descen-

---

64  Matthew 26:16
65  Mark 14:18
66  Luke 22:48

dant of David. His early followers *wanted* him to be of Davidic ancestry in order to prove he was the Messiah. The genealogies of Matthew and Luke are evidence of this, but their contradictions make them unreliable.

There are other reasons for disbelieving Jesus' Davidic ancestry. Besides the fact that Galileans were not ethnic Jews who could claim to be descended from Abraham, Jesus never claimed to be the exception. In John a crowd is divided between believing Jesus is the messiah or rejecting him:

> [40] When the people heard Jesus, some said, "This is indeed the prophet." [41] Others said, "He is the messiah." Still others said, "The messiah cannot come from Galilee, can he? [42] Doesn't the scripture say that the messiah will come from the house of David and from Bethlehem, David's village?" [43] And so the crowd was divided about Jesus. [44] Some wanted to arrest him, but no one laid hands on him.[67]

This dispute makes sense only if people knew that Jesus did *not* descend from David or come from Bethlehem.

In another account Jesus is accused of being born of fornication and having a devil, while the Pharisees had Abraham as their father.

> [39] [The Jews] answered [Jesus], "Abraham is our father."
>
> Jesus said to them, "If you were children of Abraham, you would do the deeds of Abraham. [40] But now you want to kill me, when I have told you the truth that I heard from God. That is not what Abraham did. [41] You are certainly doing the same as your father does."
>
> They said to him, "We are not born from fornication; we have only one father, [and that is] God."[68]

---

67  John 7:40-44
68  John 8:39-41

This not about the Jews suspecting that Jesus was illegitimate, perhaps having heard rumors that Joseph was not his real father. Even if he were illegitimate, that would not keep him from being a descendant of Abraham. The Jews in this story, claiming their superiority because Abraham was their father, were attacking Jesus not with a suspicion of illegitimacy, but because of his *ancestry*. The accusation is reasonable only if Jesus was, like all Galileans, *not* an ethnic Jew; but it would be readily refuted if Jesus could trace his ancestry to David.

Mark gives this account of what Jesus taught about David and the messiah:

> 35 As Jesus was teaching in the temple, he asked, "Why do the scribes say that the Messiah is the son of David? 36 By the holy spirit David himself said, 'The Lord said to my Lord, "Sit at my right hand, until I make your enemies your footstool."' 37 And so David himself calls him Lord; how, then, can he be his son?" And the large crowd was delighted to hear him.[69]

In other words, the Messiah would *not* be a son of David.

As much as the early Christians desired to make Jesus a descendant of David born in Bethlehem, the Gospels point in the opposite direction, a position the first followers would not have made up. And if he was not from David, then neither could he have claimed royal blood to be king of Israel.

## Pilate: "Are you a king?"

What, then, moved Pilate to ask Jesus if he was a king? Mark says that his accusers gave false testimony,[70] and Luke expands on this by adding accusations of perverting the nation, forbidding the payment of taxes to Rome, and saying that he was the messiah and a king.[71] Being a king was the one accusation that Pilate focused on when he questioned Jesus. We

---

69  Mark 12:35-37
70  Mark 14:56
71  Luke 23:2

*False Questions*

cannot know for certain, since there were no witnesses present, but it is the way the evangelists tell the story.

In every passion account Pilate questions Jesus about claiming to be king. Jesus' reply may seem ambiguous, "You say so," but even if it means yes, Pilate dismissed the charges and found no fault in Jesus, nor any crime to have been committed.

As unlikely as this seems, Pilate took Jesus' side *against* the Jewish leaders. Pilate's mistrust of them is seldom discussed, but it is an essential part of the story and can account for why Pilate judged as he did. He finally concluded that Jesus had really been handed over out of jealousy.[72]

Here we can read between the lines. These leaders had, on their own, hunted down and arrested a teacher with no known record of revolutionary activity or of being a public nuisance. Pilate surely would have asked himself why these Jewish leaders were suddenly showing such extraordinary patriotism and concern for Roman authority. Such action on the part of the high priests must have been rare, and Pilate must have been suspicious of these leaders from the beginning.

Pilate's attitude toward Jesus' accusers displayed no gratitude, trust or friendliness, and defendants usually win a not-guilty verdict whenever the prosecution cannot be trusted.

## Our Answer

In spite of his conviction — and this is the way all the evangelists tell the story — he gave in and turned Jesus over to be crucified. We return now to our question, *what were the legal charges against Jesus?* Our answer: *there were no legitimate legal charges*. Pilate rejected all the accusations. Regardless, he sentenced him to death, so that he was totally responsible. But the theories that Jesus was put to death because he was part of a rebel movement, or because it came to light that he had secretly claimed to be a king, lack evidence.

---

72  Mark 15:10

## The Sign Above the Cross

Pilate's character and state of mind can be deduced from the sign placed atop Jesus' crucifix, "Jesus of Nazareth, King of the Jews." Since Pilate dismissed the accusation that Jesus claimed to be a king, why did he erect the sign?

My own hypothesis is this: Since Pilate judged Jesus to be innocent, his primary motive would not have been to ridicule Jesus. Instead, Pilate must have been annoyed, if not angry, with the chief priests and leaders who brought the false charges. Giving in to them does not mean respecting them. After the sign was erected, the Jewish leaders asked Pilate to change it to read, "*He said*, 'I am the king of the Jews.'" Pilate refused: "What I have written, I have written."[73]

Pilate would have been familiar with Jewish customs and beliefs. He would have known that their messiah and king had to be a son of David. If Pilate was angry with the Jewish leaders — as I believe he was — and if the sign was against their wishes — as the Gospel of John says it was — then Pilate posted the sign to mock not Jesus but his accusers.

## The Release of Jesus' Body

The last part of the passion that some modern scholars question is whether Pilate would have let the body be taken down from the cross early and given to Joseph of Arimathea, when bodies were customarily left on the cross for days after one died, and then thrown into a common grave. On one hand, we must question whether biblical details can fit into the historical customs of their time. On the other hand, the researcher's task is also to ascertain whether details that may seem unusual may have an alternative explanation. A biblical scholar should first explain the text, not explain it away.

Those who assert that Jesus' body had to be left on the cross and thrown into a common grave days (or weeks?) later create a new problem. Yes, the Romans almost always let the bodies of crucified victims

---

73  John 19:21

decay on their crosses until they rotted. Only then would they be taken down and buried. If this is what happened to Jesus, his body would have still been on the cross on the Sunday he was declared to have been raised, and for even much longer. This would have been known by all the inhabitants of Jerusalem, the Twelve and all the followers of Jesus. Why, then, would any of them have invented a tradition that the risen Christ was witnessed while his body was still on the cross?

The teaching that Jesus was raised on the third day was an extremely old tradition, as Paul relates:

> [3]I passed on to you something most important, which I myself received, that Christ died for our sins, according to the scriptures; [4]and that he was buried, then raised on the third day according to the scriptures; [5]and also that he appeared to Cephas, then to the twelve. [6]Then he was seen by more than five hundred of us at the same time — most of whom are still alive, although some have died. [7]Then he was seen by James, and afterward by all the apostles. [8]Last of all he was also seen by me, as to one born outside the normal time.[74]

Paul says that he passed on to the Corinthians what he himself received. This is a formula stating a tradition that was given to him. The latest he could have received this teaching is 57 C.E., since First Corinthians was written between 53 and 57 C.E. But he must have taught this to the Corinthians earlier than then, when he established the church in Corinth. However, the most likely time for his being instructed in the details of Jesus' resurrection and appearances would be when he was converted, between 35 and 38 C.E. Whenever we choose to date the information Paul received, it had to have been part of the earliest apostolic teaching, from long before the Gospels were written. Even if Paul had not been instructed in this doctrine until the year 50, it would have been hard for the Twelve or others to create it when people who

---

74   First Corinthians 15:3-8

were still alive could recall that Jesus' body was still on the cross on the Sunday after the crucifixion.

## Release of the Body

On the part of Joseph of Arimathea, the request makes sense. Jews were to be buried within twenty-four hours of dying, but they could not be buried on the Sabbath, which began at sundown. Joseph had but a few hours in which to fulfill the law.

But why would Pilate release the body? Consider a possible motive. He had just executed a man he had judged innocent. He disliked those who caused all the trouble. Although to hand over the body of Jesus would have been exceptional, the actions of the high priests in arresting a little known (at least to Pilate) teacher and turning him over to Pilate under the pretense of loyalty to Rome were also exceptional. He could have let Joseph of Arimathea have the body out of spite for Jesus' accusers. This theory is, in my opinion, just as reasonable as saying that Jesus' body had to be left on a cross and buried in a common grave because "that is the way it always happened."

The strongest argument against my hypothesis is that the evangelists wanted to blame Jesus' execution on the Jews and absolve Pilate, so that we are left with only a theological story with no reliable history. I offer my position as equally tenable.

## The Burial

The details of Jesus' burial match up with what archeology has revealed about customs in first century Jerusalem. As a wealthy Jew, Joseph of Arimathea would have had a mausoleum for family burial. These monuments were most often carved into rock on a hillside, with two or more stone pillars and a triangular or pyramidal top. Between the pillars was a doorway, and a round stone could be rolled to open or close access to the doorway.

Upon entering there would be a room on the right and a room on the left. One was to hold bodies until only bones remained. The other was to contain all the bones, piled together, from the other room. In the room where the bodies were first placed, there would be a series of pedestals raised off the floor. Each pedestal was hollowed out on the top with a space wide enough and long enough to hold one human body. This hollowed out space was called a *loculus* (plural, *loculi*) and would resemble a niche in a wall, except that it was lying horizontal and raised off the floor.

This was the kind of mausoleum that would have belonged to Joseph of Arimathea. When the Scripture states that it was a tomb in which no one had yet been laid, it is usually understood that no one had yet been placed in the mausoleum. However, the statement could, though less likely, be interpreted to mean that no one had yet been laid in the loculus where Jesus was placed. Since the mausoleum was a family tomb, it is possible that others had been laid in some of the other loculi.

Whatever happened in the arrest and burial has no bearing on whether Jesus was raised from the dead.

CHAPTER 5

# Sin and Salvation

The conviction that God resurrected Jesus caused a radical change in the theological perspective of the disciples. Paul, who had been persecuting Jesus' followers, reversed his beliefs and accepted Jesus as God's Messiah. In doing so, *he was challenged by the question of why a sinless agent of God would die as a criminal.* For him, death and sin went together. Death came into the world as a punishment for Adam's sin. He saw sin and death as cosmic powers that held sway over the world.

If Jesus had been raised from the dead, then he had conquered death; and if he had conquered death, he had conquered sin as well. He had to figure out why the Messiah, who was to be without sin, should suffer death, which was a penalty for sin. His conclusion was that Jesus did not die for his own sins, but for the sins of others.

So far so good. Jesus died to save people from their sins. Since people were still dying, resurrection from the dead was pushed into the future to coincide with the second coming. But people had to be saved from sin at once, lest they be condemned at the second coming, which could arrive at any moment.

If the apostolic community pondered how the merits of Jesus' death were to be bestowed on the rest of humanity, their solution was simple: just accept the gift. This required preaching on the part of the first disciples, and then one could be saved by hearing the message, *believing,* and accepting forgiveness — and, of course, by abandoning sin and living a just life.

Thus began the change from believing Jesus to believing *in* Jesus. What Jesus taught receded to the background; who Jesus was became essential. In the Gospels, when Jesus said, "Your faith has saved you," the word for faith meant "steadfastness" or "faithfulness." By the middle of the second century that word came to mean a list of doctrines.

The conversion of a Gentile eventually required two steps which were combined into the same ritual: a profession of faith (or belief *in* something) and baptism. And so we will discuss the forgiveness of sin 1) through baptism, 2) through a profession of faith or by accepting Jesus and 3) after conversion.

## A. Baptism and Forgiveness

Christians are initiated through baptism, but there is no agreement over what baptism does. Some say it forgives original sin (passed down from Adam and Eve) along with personal sin. Some think it makes one a member of a specific community or church; others say it unites one with all Christians. Baptism is often required to receive communion or other sacraments. Many believe one is not fully Christian or "saved" without baptism. These ideas are theological conclusions. Here I will explore what baptism meant for the first Christians. Our question is, *how are sins forgiven in baptism?*

Over a century before the time of Jesus, the Qumran community practiced a form of baptism or ritual bathing, but there is no historical link between this practice and Christian baptism. Consequently, we will begin with another Jewish ritual practiced in the time of Jesus.

### Jewish Proselyte Baptism

Before the appearance of John the Baptist, Gentile converts to Judaism, called *proselytes*, were baptized. Proselytes were distinguished from *God fearers*, who were Gentiles who accepted the one Jewish God and observed some Jewish rites, but did not accept circumcision or Judaism in its entirety; they remained Gentiles. A proselyte, on the other hand, was no longer a Gentile, but a member of the Jewish religion.

When a Gentile wanted to embrace Judaism, that person, if male, would have to be circumcised. Often the convert would come to Jerusalem, where a special sacrifice would be offered in the temple. While in Jerusalem the proselyte would usually be baptized in the pool of Siloam.[75] The moment of conversion, which was not tied to a specific moment such as circumcision or baptism, changed the proselyte into a "new-born infant," meaning that one had received forgiveness of sin and shared in the blessing of salvation promised to the nation of Israel.

---

75 Jeremias, Joachim, *Jerusalem in the Time of Jesus,* Fortress Press, Philadelphia, 1975, page 320.

We must not read Christian ideas into Judaic baptism. Aside from temple sacrifices, Judaism had no individual rites to seek forgiveness. Instead, Israelites were exhorted to repent and do penance, such as fasting, or putting on sackcloth and ashes, for their sins. Jews would hardly have invented a ritual such as baptism for converts to obtain forgiveness when they had no equivalent ritual for themselves. Consequently, baptism must have been a ritual to express a cleansing of the body as a sign of the cleansing of the whole person, body and soul, effected by one's conversion.

Becoming a proselyte was a one-time event, and only for *converts* to Judaism. Once one's conversion was complete, the proselyte was obligated to follow the Jewish Law or Torah, and was also entitled to receive needed charity.

Proselytes were totally Jewish in the religious sense, but they — and their offspring — were still not equal to the descendants of Abraham. Baptism added no spiritual advantage to the proselyte and could only have been a ritual to help strengthen one's commitment.

## The Baptism of John the Baptist

John the Baptist challenged those who thought they were superior because of Abrahamitic ancestry.

> [7] But when [John] saw many Pharisees and Sadducees coming for baptism, he said to them, "You brood of snakes! Who warned you to run away from the coming wrath? [8] Bear good works that show true repentance. [9] Do not be presumptuous and say to yourselves, 'Our father is Abraham.' Let me tell you, God can raise up children for Abraham from these stones. [10] And right now the ax is placed at the root of the trees; therefore every tree that does not produce good fruit is going to be cut down and tossed into the fire."[76]

John's actions were as radical as his words. He imitated the baptismal rite undergone by proselytes and opened it up to those already Jews. Just as the proselyte had to undergo a change of heart or spirit of repentance,

---

76  Matthew 3:7-10

John expected his baptismal candidates to approach only *after* already repenting for their sins.

Besides accounts from the Gospel of John, we have the testimony of Josephus:

> "the washing [with water] would be acceptable...supposing still that the soul was thoroughly purified beforehand by righteousness."[77]

Josephus gives us this theological interpretation of John's baptism: 1) Those coming for baptism would already be purified spiritually by their righteousness or repentance. 2) Baptism was for the (ritual) purification of the body, provided that one had *already* truly repented. Consequently, John's baptism was both *symbolic* of repentance and *a cleansing of the body*, or an act symbolizing the purification of the total person.

As in the baptism of a proselyte, in John's baptism forgiveness or spiritual change of heart takes place *before* the ritual, which is a bodily purification completing the process of conversion.

Some authors reject the testimony of Josephus, asserting that John's baptism was in competition with temple sacrifices as a means to atone for sin, and in a less expensive way. Their argument goes something like this:

> *The activity of John in the desert was a symbol of ancient Israel baptized in the Jordan (symbolic of the Red Sea), crossing over the water from the desert and then returning to the Promised Land.* (To conclude that John's baptism atoned for sin, I presume that baptized people returning to the Promised Land were imagined in some way as a new Israel with their sins washed away.)

---

77 *The New Complete Works of Josephus,* Translated by William Whiston, Commentary by Paul L. Maier, Kregel Publications, Grand Rapids, MI, 1999, Jewish Antiquities, Book 18, Chapter 5, Paragraph 2, page 595.

> *The symbolism resembled the activities of others posing as prophets shortly before John's time. Herod's arrest of John was a political reaction to the fear that John's actions would turn from symbolic to actual uprisings in the country.*

There are several reasons for rejecting this and similar theories: 1) While John may have been seen as just one more false prophet who was about to disrupt the peace, there is no reason to assume a religious symbolism of a cleansed people returning to the Promised Land. 2) Even if John's baptism was a means to atone for sin, the thought that it was in competition with temple sacrifices has nothing to support it. 3) Herod may have considered John a political nuisance, but without further information we do not know how he interpreted John's activities.

These ideas have often appeared in literature also advocating that Jesus was a political activist or peasant rebel and that John had similar leanings. As a result, I am suspicious of the authors' bias.

John's baptism must be understood in the context of apocalypticism. Some Jews in his time could not understand why they suffered under the domination of a foreign power, even though they were doing their best to keep the Torah. Why hadn't God kept the promises made to Abraham? They concluded that God had allowed evil to prevail for a limited time, but this time was soon coming to an end. John expressed this view of the immediate judgment of God.

> "And right now the ax is placed at the root of the trees; therefore every tree that does not produce good fruit is going to be cut down and tossed into the fire."[78]

Jesus too taught that the kingdom was about to come in the immediate future:

---

78  Matthew 3:10

> ¹ And Jesus said to them, "Amen (Indeed) I say to you, there are some standing here who will not taste death until they see the kingdom of God coming in power."[79]

After the resurrection, Christians still expected Jesus to return in the near future. This was stated by Paul in First Thessalonians[80] and at the end of the book of Revelation.

John's baptism, then, was a sign of repentance in preparation for God's imminent judgment.

## Christian Baptism

An examination of the nature of Christian baptism begins with the relationship between John the Baptist and Jesus. That Jesus was baptized by John is beyond doubt, since this was an embarrassment to the first Christians. The Gospels consistently state that Jesus is greater than John: Luke tells of the miraculous birth of John, but he makes the virgin birth of Jesus even greater. John himself is said to have recognized Jesus as the greater. And just as Jesus was superior to John, so baptism in Jesus' name was superior to John's. Those who had received John's baptism had to be baptized again in the name of Jesus.[81]

We can also compare Christian baptism with John's baptism and with that of proselytes. A common element in all three is that they were a one-time event.

Baptism of proselytes and that of John were Jewish rituals, whereas the apostles extended Christian baptism to Gentiles who did not become Jews.

Proselytes and John's followers had to go to a certain place, such as Jerusalem or the Jordan River. The apostles baptized wherever their converts were at the time.

---

79  Mark 9:1
80  First Thessalonians 4:13-18
81  Acts 18-19

For both proselyte and Johannine baptism the candidate was presumed, even *required*, to approach only after having experienced spiritual conversion. In both instances one was *already forgiven*, and baptism was a ritual washing of the body to complete or symbolize the conversion of the whole person. A similar perspective of Christian baptism is found in First Peter:

> [18]For Christ suffered once for sins, the just one for the unjust, to bring us to God — put to death in the flesh, but made alive in the spirit, [19]And by the spirit he went and preached to the spirits in prison, [20]who a long time ago disobeyed when God waited patiently in the days of Noah, during the construction of the ark, in which just a few — that is, eight persons — were saved through water. [21]That water foreshadowed baptism, which now saves us, not as a washing of dirt off the body, but as a pledge and an appeal to God for a good conscience, through the resurrection of Jesus Christ, [22]who has gone into heaven and is at God's right hand, with angels, authorities, and powers made to submit to him.[82]

This is the only passage in the New Testament that defines baptism, or tells us *what baptism is*. The phrase "a pledge and an appeal to God for a good conscience" is my translation of a wording with a double meaning: "an appeal to God for a good conscience" can also be translated "a pledge to God from a good conscience." In either case the spiritual conversion of the one baptized is required for baptism. Therefore, the effects attributed to baptism come from the disposition of the candidate. If one does not have the proper disposition, then baptism is an empty ceremony. The passage also adds that baptism is *not* a washing or removal of dirt from the body.

First Peter tells us that the good conscience of the Christian comes "through the resurrection of Jesus Christ." The superiority of Christian baptism is described in various ways in Acts and in Paul's letters, where

---

82 First Peter 3:18-22

it is called baptism "in the holy spirit,"[83] baptism "in the name of Jesus" and baptism "into Jesus' death." A convert's good conscience relied upon Jesus' death and resurrection.

The understanding of relying on Jesus' merits and salvific action for a good conscience is similar to the way Jews believed that they relied on the good works and merits of Abraham. In the book of Revelation we find these perspectives combined: We are saved by the blood of the Lamb, but our salvation still comes through Israel, the mother of the Messiah.

## Christian Baptism: Jesus' Teaching

After Jesus is baptized, the Gospel of John reports that he spent time with his disciples and baptized.[84] The followers of John the Baptist, who was nearby, complained that people were going to Jesus rather than to John. After this one instance we have no other account of Jesus baptizing. He was constantly moving from place to place, and the lack of a plentiful water supply would have made a baptismal ministry difficult.

The Synoptic Gospels say nothing about Jesus ever baptizing, and consequently it is highly unlikely that he carried on a baptismal ministry. After John the Baptist was executed, Jesus apparently made a complete split with John's movement and carried on his own preaching ministry.

Many churches teach that Jesus himself instituted baptism:

> [16]Then the eleven disciples departed for Galilee, to the mountain where Jesus had told them to go. [17]When they saw him, they worshiped him; but some were doubtful. [18]And Jesus came and told them, "All authority, in heaven and on earth, has been given to me. [19]Go therefore and make disciples of all nations, baptizing them in the name of the father and of the son and of the holy spirit, [20]teaching them to obey all that I have commanded you. And behold, I am with you always, to the end of the age."[85]

---

83  The words "holy spirit" are not capitalized in the Greek text.
84  John 3:22
85  Matthew 28:16-20. The words "father," "son" and "holy spirit" are not capitalized in the Greek.

*False Questions*

Matthew's story presents Jesus as using a formula for baptism — "in the name of the Father and of the Son and of the Holy Spirit" — which, according to Acts and Paul, was not used immediately after Jesus died. If Jesus explicitly commanded the use of the formula recorded in Matthew, then we have to explain why other formulas, such as "in the name of Jesus," were used. Consequently, Jesus' command at the end of Matthew is best understood as an expression of a practice developed sometime after Jesus died and placed on Jesus' lips in the resurrection narrative.

In spite of the resurrection story containing the evangelical command in Matthew, it is this evangelist who pictures Jesus not as rejecting Judaism, but as thoroughly Jewish, as the new Moses, and as fulfilling the Law. Never in the Gospels did Jesus ever reject any part of Judaism or advocate substituting Judaism with a new religion. Any attempt to reform Judaism would have been an attempt to preserve it.

The Gospel passage most frequently quoted to prove that Jesus demanded baptism to be saved is, "No one can see the kingdom of God without being born again ... No one can enter the kingdom of God without being born of water and spirit."[86] The entire passage in John 3 is a conversation between Jesus and Nicodemus. In several instances in this story there is a play on words, and the most noted is the use of the Greek word *anothen,* which means either "again," which is the way Nicodemus understands it, or "from above," which is the way Jesus intended. Because this passage makes sense only with the word play in Greek, whereas Jesus and Nicodemus spoke Aramaic, Scripture scholars today reject John 3:3-5 as an authentic saying of Jesus. Instead, the whole conversation was created by the evangelist to express his own theological views.

Since Jesus lived and died a faithful Jew, he would not have instituted a new religion or new religious rituals. Baptism must have been instituted after he died. Why?

---

86 John 3:3-5

## Christian Baptism: Apostolic Teaching and Practice

The Acts of the Apostles says that the apostles baptized three thousand Jewish pilgrims on Pentecost. That the apostles did so is questionable; it would seem that Jews could accept Jesus or anyone else as messiah without any kind of ritual.

After the resurrection, there were three groups of people who accepted Jesus as the Messiah. The first are the apostles and those who followed Jesus until the time of his crucifixion, and all those who continued to believe in him after the resurrection. We are not aware that any of these were baptized unless by John.

The second group comprises Jews who came to accept Jesus as Messiah after the resurrection. If one sees baptism as a *conversion to a new religion*, then the baptism of these Jews makes no sense. James and the apostles remained faithful to Judaism and would have thought of Jesus as the *Jewish* Messiah, since Jesus and James lived and died as faithful Jews. While we know of the demands of some that Gentiles be circumcised, we know of no equivalent demand that Jews be baptized.

If, however, baptism was believed to be a ritualized statement of one's commitment to Christ, then *maybe* the apostles, along with the original followers of Jesus, might have told new Jewish believers to be baptized. This would make sense if these new converts thought of this new baptism in the same way as they thought of the baptism of John, but not if they saw it as an entry into a new religion. It also would have been reasonable for the apostles to call this "baptism in the name of Jesus" to distinguish it from the baptism of John.

The third group would be Gentile converts. The apostles might have felt a need for some way to initiate these converts, and baptism would have been a natural choice, in imitation of both proselyte baptism and the baptism of John. This new ceremony could have been done "in the name of Jesus" to distinguish it from the other two forms of baptism.

In proselyte baptism, in John's baptism, in Christian baptism as defined in First Peter, and in Jesus' teachings, the one absolute requirement is one's proper disposition. Perhaps the best word to describe this disposition is *metanoia,* meaning a change in one's way of thinking, and usually translated in the Gospels as repentance.

Jesus required *metanoia* or a change in one's way of thinking to enter God's kingdom, but he prescribed no ritual, not even prayers to be said aloud, nor other conditions, such as ancestry, sacrifice, penitential acts or dogmas. Neither do we find such rituals anywhere in the Old Testament, but only a change of heart.

Neither is baptism a ritual to bestow forgiveness. If sins were forgiven through any kind of ceremony, it would be a novelty in both the Old and New Testaments.

## Our Answer

We can now return to the question at the beginning of this section, *how are sins forgiven in baptism?* There is no answer, because *sins are not forgiven in or through baptism.*

# B. Belief and Forgiveness

Early in Christian history correct belief was deemed essential for salvation:

> [Jesus said to the eleven,] "Whoever believes and is baptized will be saved, but whoever does not believe will be condemned."[87]

This verse, however, cannot be attributed to Jesus, and not even to the pen of Mark, since his Gospel originally ended at chapter 16, verse 8. Verses after that were added long after Mark was first written, probably because the scribes copying it thought it ended too abruptly, without any resurrection appearances.

The apostle Paul demanded that those he taught accept only what he taught, and he severely condemned anyone who preached a different message.

In the second century each church claimed to have the one orthodox doctrine, while condemning other opinions as heresies.

## The Creed

In the Catholic Church baptism is always preceded by a profession of faith. In some Christian denominations one is saved by accepting Christ as one's personal savior. Nearly every Christian church uses the Apostles' Creed. In some churches this creed is recited at all Sunday services. For others it may not be in regular use, but will be found in their hymnals or prayer books. Respect for this creed is based on the belief that it goes back to the earliest Christian times, although it is no longer believed to originate with the twelve apostles; it did not receive its name until the fourth century.

The Catholic Church uses the Nicene Creed in its Sunday masses, but the Apostles' Creed is used at other times, such as in saying the rosary. The following is a Catholic version of this creed:

---

87  Mark 16:16

> I believe in God, the Father almighty, Creator of heaven and earth, and in Jesus Christ, his only Son, our Lord, who was conceived by the Holy Spirit,
> born of the Virgin Mary, suffered under Pontius Pilate, was crucified, died and was buried;
> he descended into hell; on the third day he rose again from the dead;
> he ascended into heaven, and is seated at the right hand of God the Father almighty; from there he will come to judge the living and the dead.
> I believe in the Holy Spirit, the holy catholic Church, the communion of saints, the forgiveness of sins, the resurrection of the body, and life everlasting.
> Amen.

This creed summarizes Christian beliefs. At the same time, it contains almost nothing of what Jesus taught.

If it is true that we must believe in Jesus or in certain doctrines in order to be saved from sin, then we have to answer our second question, *how are sins forgiven by a profession of faith or by accepting Jesus as Messiah or Savior?* To answer, I will examine what Jesus himself taught about forgiveness.

## The Parable of the Unjust Servant

Luke relates a parable told by Jesus as an illustration of the necessity to forgive:

> [21]Then Peter came to him and said, "If my brother or sister sins against me, how many times should I forgive? Up to seven times?" [22]Jesus said to him, "I wouldn't say seven times, but seventy times seven times.
>
> [23]"Consequently, the heavenly kingdom is like a king who wanted to settle accounts with his servants. [24]And when he began the audit, a man was brought to him with a debt of millions [literally, ten thousand talents]. [25]But since he could not pay, the ruler gave the order for him, his wife and children, and all he had to be sold to make payment. [26]The servant fell to his knees before him. 'Be patient with me,' he said, 'and I will pay back everything.' [27]The

servant's master took pity on him, released him, and forgave the debt.

²⁸"But as the servant went out, he found a coworker who owed him a few dollars [literally, a hundred denarii]. He seized him and grabbed him by the throat. He said, 'Pay me what you owe.' ²⁹His coworker dropped down before his feet and begged him, 'Be patient with me, and I will pay you.' ³⁰And he refused, but instead went out and had the man put in jail until he paid the debt.

³¹"When other coworkers saw what had happened, they were torn apart and went to tell their master what had happened. ³²'You wicked servant,' he said, 'I forgave your entire debt because you begged me to. ³³Shouldn't you have also had pity on your coworker, just as I had pity on you?' ³⁴In his anger the ruler handed him over to the torturers until he paid him back everything he owed.

³⁵"And this is how my heavenly Father will act toward each one of you if you do not forgive your brother and sister from your heart."[88]

Jesus draws a clear picture of God's forgiveness: When we ask to be forgiven, God readily and mercifully grants it. There is only one condition, which is that we in turn forgive those who have wronged us. We ourselves, then, are the only ones who can keep the gift of forgiveness from being effective, and it is by refusing to pass the gift on to others.

We must remember Jesus' audience. He was not preaching to baptized Christians or to Gentiles about to be converted. He spoke to his own people, who were not Christians, but non-baptized Jews. He was also preaching about God's forgiveness *before* he was supposed to have won forgiveness for sin by his death on the cross.

## The Woman with the Alabaster Jar

Another Gospel story is that of the woman with the alabaster jar of ointment:

---

[88] Matthew 18:21-35

## False Questions

³⁶One of the Pharisees invited Jesus to eat with him. He went to the Pharisee's house and took his place at table. ³⁷A woman in the city, a sinner, had learned that he was eating in the Pharisee's house, and she brought an alabaster jar of ointment. ³⁸She stood behind him at his feet, crying. Her tears fell on his feet, and she wiped them with her hair, kissing his feet and anointing them with the ointment.

³⁹Now when the Pharisee, his host, saw this, he said to himself, "If this man were a prophet, he would know who and what kind of person this is who touches him, and that she is a sinner."

⁴⁰Jesus confronted him, "Simon, I have something to say to you."

⁴¹He replied, "Teacher, speak."

"There were two persons in debt to one creditor. One owed five hundred denarii, and the other, fifty. ⁴²When they lacked enough to pay him back, he canceled both debts. Now which one will love him more?"

⁴³Simon answered, "I guess the one who was released from the bigger debt."

Jesus said to him, "You have judged correctly." ⁴⁴And turning to the woman, he said to Simon, "Do you see this woman? I entered your house, and you offered me no water for my feet, but she has moistened my feet with her tears and wiped them dry with her hair. ⁴⁵You did not give me a kiss, but she has not stopped kissing my feet ever since she came in. ⁴⁶Neither did you anoint my head with oil, but with ointment she has anointed my feet. ⁴⁷Consequently, I tell you, know that her many sins have been forgiven her, for she shows so much love. But whoever is forgiven less, loves less." ⁴⁸And he said to the woman, "Your sins have been forgiven."

⁴⁹And those who were also at the table began to say to each other, "Who is this who even forgives sin?"

⁵⁰But he said to the woman, "Your faith has saved you. Go in peace."[89]

---

[89] Luke 7:36-50

Verse 47 is significant; here is another rendering:

> ⁴⁷"Therefore, I say this to you: her many sins are forgiven her; as a result, she has loved much. But the one for whom less is forgiven, loves less."

Jesus reverses the usual order of acts that take place when God forgives: We expect that first one must be sorry for transgressions or return to loving God, and only afterward does God forgive. Instead, Jesus asserts that first God forgives, and then one loves. This is clear from verse 47, "whoever is forgiven less, loves less."

The story contradicts the notion that God waits for anything on our part before forgiving us, whether it be sorrow, love, baptism, confession, or even Jesus' death on the cross. God always forgives, whether or not we ask for it. Of course, we have to accept it. But forgiveness is always there for us.

## The Lord's Prayer

Most Christians say the Lord's Prayer, some frequently, others not so much. One of the petitions is "Forgive us our trespasses as we forgive those who trespass against us." This petition, found in both Matthew and Luke and presented as a prayer Jesus taught, has the same meaning as the parable of the unjust steward.[90] We ask that God forgive us in the same way as we forgive others; if we forgive, God forgives us, but if we do not forgive, we are blocking forgiveness from God:

> ¹⁴For if you forgive others their offenses, your heavenly Father will also forgive you. ¹⁵But if you do not forgive those who offend you, neither will your Father forgive your offenses.[91]

## Our Answer

Jesus taught us that God always forgives, even before we ask for forgiveness, and the only obstacle to our receiving this gift is our refusal

---

90  Matthew 18:23-35
91  Matthew 6:14-15

to pass it on to others. The answer to our second question on forgiveness, *how are sins forgiven by a profession of faith or by accepting Jesus as Savior?* is clear. *It is a false assumption that belief or accepting Jesus is a requirement for forgiveness*, and therefore these conditions are irrelevant.

God always forgives. We accept the gift. We pass the gift on by forgiving just as generously. It's that simple.

## C. Forgiveness in Christian Churches

Right after Jesus tells the Twelve how to punish a guilty party by removal from the community and how to forgive by readmittance, Peter asks him how often one should forgive.

> [21]Then Peter came to him and said, "If my brother or sister sins against me, how many times should I forgive? Up to seven times?"
>
> [22]Jesus said to him, "I wouldn't say seven times, but seventy times seven times.[92]

Jesus' norm is to forgive seventy times seven times, meaning to keep on forgiving more than you can count. Our question for this section is, *how did Christian churches forgive sinners after their conversion?*

### Public Penance

Because the penalties for grave crimes were public, the offender had to make some kind of public admission of guilt, probably to the local bishop. We can call this a confession, but it was not made in a private room or in secret, as is the practice in the Catholic Church today. And after the confession, there was no absolution. In its place was the imposition of a penalty. Forgiveness came only after the penalty was completed.

The principle for punishing and forgiving guilty Christians remained the same for centuries, but the practice itself changed over time. By today's standards, the discipline of the first five or six centuries was extremely harsh.

In the East, Basil (c. 370) divided Christians into five categories: 1) *Mourners*, who could only stand outside the church doors and beg for prayers. 2) *Hearers*, who could stand inside the church in the narthex until the catechumens left. 3) *Fallers*, who could stand in the church nave but also had to leave with the catechumens. 4) *Bystanders*, who

---

92  Matthew 18:21-22

could stay for the entire liturgy but could not receive communion. 5) *Participants,* who could receive communion.

These are some sample penalties for certain crimes: 1) Homicide: 4 years as a mourner, 5 as a hearer, 7 as a faller and 4 as a bystander, for a total of 20 years. 2) Adultery: 4 years as a mourner, 5 as a hearer, 4 as a faller and 2 as a bystander, for a total of 15 years. 3) Theft: one year of penance if one accused oneself; two if convicted. 4) Apostasy: penance (sacrament of reconciliation) and communion only at the end of one's life.[93]

The West was equally severe. In theory all grave sins were to be submitted to the church; in practice only the three capital sins of apostasy, murder and adultery were punished. Western synods of bishops encouraged postponing confession until a mature age, since the sacrament of reconciliation could be received only once in one's lifetime.

Throughout the first five centuries there was no practice of confessing privately, of confessing lesser (venial) sins or of confessing repeatedly. Only from the sixth century on did penitential practices begin to evolve into what Catholics experience today.

## Indirect Forgiveness by Remission of Punishment

In the earliest times theologians concluded that the church could forgive sin *only indirectly* by allowing readmission to communion. When the church embraces the sinner, God also forgives. But the power to loose was still only the power to loose what the community *had itself bound.*

The beliefs and practices of Catholics today in receiving the sacrament of reconciliation are the exact opposite of what was going on in Christian churches in the first six centuries. Penance was always done publicly, as was readmittance to the community. Only the gravest sins were confessed. Reconciliation after baptism was granted only once; a second time was allowed only on one's deathbed.

Since excommunication was originally the same as being deprived of communion, there was no excommunication apart from what took

---

93  Note that apostasy was considered worse than homicide or adultery.

place in every grave sin. In other words, every mortal (or each of the three capital sins) sin was considered to result in excommunication, and a sacramental penance without excommunication was inconceivable.

Indulgences, like the sacrament of reconciliation, owe their origin to the tradition of binding and loosing. The church would impose a penalty lasting thirty days or five years, and an indulgence could be granted to take the place of that penalty. With the understanding that the church could loose from its own penalties, indulgences made sense.

Only over centuries did the Catholic Church change its belief from one of pardoning its own penalties to one of forgiving sin and punishment in God's name.

### Early Church Practice

To summarize, in the early centuries of Christianity the practice of forgiveness by the Church bore little resemblance to Jesus' command. The principle of forgiving by releasing from the penalty the Church had imposed was still observed. The command to keep on forgiving was not. Sinners were given no second chance until on their deathbed. Many prospective converts, like Constantine, delayed baptism until death was close at hand, because the rules for forgiveness were so severe.

In later centuries the Catholic Church reversed both its doctrines and its norms regarding the forgiveness of sins. In a kind of mission creep, the Church claimed not only the power to impose punishment, but also the power to forgive sins in God's name. Absolution came first and in private, and for the smallest of transgressions; then came the penance.

Neither the harshness of the first centuries nor the modern practice of confession bears any resemblance to Jesus' instructions in Matthew 18. Christians missed the point: he was teaching how to correct and rehabilitate a sinner, and about the need to forgive.

### Our Answer

Our question was, *how did Christian churches forgive sinners after their conversion?* History tells us that the Christian churches did *not* practice Jesus' command to forgive seventy times seven. They never *directly* forgave baptized Christians who were guilty of serious crimes, but only forgave punishments they had imposed. And the churches were stingy in granting pardon. Maybe individual Christians took Jesus' command to keep on forgiving more seriously.

# CHAPTER 6

# **Spiritual Adoption**

Christians generally believe that they are children of God. According to the apostle Paul, we are God's *adopted* children, as he states in the passages below, with the pertinent words italicized:

> [12] Therefore, brothers and sisters, we are debtors not to the flesh, so that we would live according to the flesh. [13] For if you should live according to the flesh, you will die; if, however, by the spirit you put to death the deeds of the flesh, you will live. [14] For whoever are led by the spirit of God are children of God. [15] For you did not receive a spirit of slavery to be fearful again, but you received *a spirit of adoption as children*, in whom we cry out, "Abba Father." [16] For that same spirit renders testimony with our spirit that *we are children of God*. [17] But if children, then heirs, heirs indeed of God and coheirs with Christ; that is, if, in fact, we suffer together with him so that we may be glorified together with him.[94]

> [1] But I say this: as long as an heir is a child, the heir is no different than a slave, even if the owner of everything; [2] but the child will stay under guardians and caretakers until the time determined by the father. [3] And it is the same with us; while we were small, we were subjected to the elements of the world. [4] But when the fullness of time came, God sent his son, born of a woman, born under the law, [5] so that he might redeem those who were under the law, and *thus we might receive adoption as children*. [6] But since you are children, God has sent the spirit of his son into your hearts,

---

[94] Romans 8:12-17

> crying out, "Abba Father."⁷ And so you are no longer a slave, but a child; and if a child, then also an heir of [through] God.[95]

When Paul calls us *adopted* children, he is not necessarily making us inferior to natural born children. In his mind and in Roman culture, an adopted child often took precedence over the natural born, because the adopted one was *intentionally chosen*. He may have been comparing adopted Gentiles with natural born Jews. The thought that God has shown us special love because we are chosen to be God's children is appealing. In a way Paul says that we have *always* been children of God, but equivalent to slaves, because we are underage. We cannot act as children and heirs until emancipated.

The other side of this coin is that Paul asserts that there is a time when we are *not yet* children of God but slaves, perhaps to sin; and then there is a change in us, and we become God's *adopted* children. This theology became predominant in the early centuries, when the Lord's Prayer was handed over to the catechumen (one preparing for baptism) as part of the baptismal or pre-baptismal rite. This symbolized that the convert could call God "Father" only after baptism.

Our question for this chapter is, *how does one become an adopted child of God?*

To answer, we begin with what Jesus himself taught and his audience.

## The Audience and Teaching of Jesus

Galileans were truly Jews in the religious sense, but their religious roots went back only about a hundred thirty years. Their ancestors before that time were Gentiles, and their inability to claim Abrahamitic ancestry put them lower on the religious scale than the ethnic Jews living in Judea.

Jesus too was a Galilean, and this was a problem:

---

95 Galatians 4:1-7

> ⁴⁰ When the people heard Jesus, some said, "This is indeed the prophet." ⁴¹ Others said, "He is the messiah." Still others said, "The messiah cannot come from Galilee, can he? ⁴² Doesn't the scripture say that the messiah will come from the house of David and from Bethlehem, David's village?" ⁴³ And so the crowd was divided about Jesus. ⁴⁴ Some wanted to arrest him, but no one laid hands on him.[96]

Jesus also chose Galileans to be his apostles, promising them a special place in the coming kingdom:

> ²⁷Then Peter said to Jesus, "Look, we have left everything and followed you. So what are we going to have?"
>
> ²⁸Jesus answered, "Amen (Indeed) I tell you, when everything is renewed and the son of man is seated on his glorious throne, you who have followed me will also sit on twelve thrones, judging the twelve tribes of Israel. ²⁹And everyone who has left houses or brothers or sisters or father or mother or children or land, for the sake of my name, will receive a hundredfold and inherit eternal life. ³⁰But many who are first (now) will be last (then), and the last will be first."[97]

Jesus preached almost exclusively to Galileans. These were people who were loyal Jews, faithful to the Torah, but looked down upon and considered to be inferior, because Abraham was not their father. We can perhaps summarize Jesus' rebuttal of such criticism: *It doesn't matter, because God is your Father:*

> ²Jesus said to them, "When you pray, say:
> Father, may your name be revered as holy.
> May your reign come.
>
> ³Each day give us our daily bread.
>
> ⁴And forgive us our sins,

---

96  John 7:40-44
97  Matthew 19:27-30

> for we also ourselves forgive those who have wronged us.
> And do not let us fall in the time of trial."[98]

Whether it was in teaching the Lord's Prayer or a parable, when Jesus first proclaimed that God was their *Father* and they were God's *children*, his words were revolutionary, turning upside down the image they had of God and of themselves. When we read the Gospels casually, we can overlook that these Galileans who could call God Father were *not Christians*. They were *not children of Abraham*. They were *not baptized*. There had *not yet been a death on a cross*. Jesus had *not yet saved the world from sin*.

We ought to be stunned by being able to call God "Father," but tragically we take it for granted. Ancient religions also used a similar form of address, and it is also found in the Old Testament, albeit only fourteen times. But the way Jesus referred to God was without precedent — radically new — for he did not use the formal term for father but an infant's first word in Aramaic, *abba*. English equivalents might be "dada," "Daddy," or "Dad."

Jesus used *abba* when he prayed in Gethsemane, as found in Mark 14:36, and Jesus' use of this form of address is certainly the source of Paul's use of *abba* in Romans 8:15 and Galatians 4:6.[99] The familiarity and tenderness of this childlike word is lost in translation when we call God "Father." To call God "Father" might have been seen as normal to Jesus' hearers, but when he used *abba*, they would have been shocked. "No Jew would have dared to address God in this manner."[100]

## What Happens at Conversion

The Galileans were God's children before Jesus told them it was so; they were just not yet aware of it. If, then, we are already children of God before our conversion, what happens to one spiritually when one is

---

98  Luke 11:2-4
99  Jeremias, Joachim, *The Lord's Prayer*, Fortress Press, Philadelphia, 1964, pages 17-22.
100 *Ibid.* pages 19-20.

*Spiritual Adoption*

converted? Jesus describes the conversion process in the parable of the prodigal:

> [11]And Jesus said, "A certain man had two sons. [12]And the younger of them said to the father, 'Father, give me the part that is coming to me.' So he divided his belongings between them. [13]And several days later, after gathering everything together, the younger son left for a distant country, and there he threw away his wealth on carefree living. [14]And when he had spent everything, a severe famine broke out throughout the country, and he began to be in need. [15]So he went and took a job with a citizen of that country, who sent him into his fields to feed pigs. [16]And he wanted so much just to fill his stomach with the husks the pigs were eating, but no one gave him a thing.
>
> [17]"But when he turned within himself, he said, 'How many of my father's hired help have more than enough food, and here I am starving to death. [18]I am going to take off and go to my father and say to him, "Father, I have sinned against heaven and before you. [19]I no longer deserve to be called your son. Put me to work as one of your hired help."' [20]So he took off and came to his father. But while he was still in the distance, his father saw him, felt compassionate toward him, took off running, hugged him around the neck, and kissed him. [21]The son said to him, 'Father, I have sinned against heaven and before you. I no longer deserve to be called your son.'
>
> [22]"But the father said to the hired help, 'Hurry! Get the best robe and put it on him. And put a ring on his finger and shoes on his feet. [23]Go get the fattened calf, butcher it, and let's eat and celebrate. [24]For this son of mine was dead and is living again. He was lost and is found.' So they began the celebration.
>
> [25]"Now the older son was in the field. When he came close to the house, he heard music and dancing. [26]And he called one of the employees and asked what was happening. [27]The employee told him, 'Your brother is here, and your father has butchered the fattened calf, because he has returned safe and sound.'
>
> [28]"But he was angry and would not go in. So his father came out and implored him. [29]But he replied and said to his father, 'You know, I have been serving you for so many years without ever going against your wishes. And yet you have never given me as much as a kid for me to party with my friends. [30]But when this son

of yours, who has thrown away your belongings on prostitutes returns home, you butcher the fattened calf for him.'

[31]"Son,' the father said, 'we are always together, and all I have is yours. [32]But we had to celebrate and be joyful, because this brother of yours was dead and is living again. He was lost and is found.'"[101]

The turning point of the parable comes in verse 17, "when he turned within himself." Different English versions of the Bible translate this in various ways, such as "when he came to himself," or "when he came to his senses." The prodigal was always his father's son, but he had forgotten his father and where he came from. His conversion was not a process of becoming a son, but of *remembering who he was and who he always had been*. In remembering who he was, he was no longer dead, but was living again, as the final line of the parable tells us. It is in this sense that one can be said to be "born again."

## Our Answer

Our question was, *how does one become an adopted child of God?* The fallacy is the belief that at one time or another we are not God's children. *We always were God's children and we always will be God's children.* Our conversion, whether expressed by baptism or some other way, is a process of remembering who we always were and always will be.

We are not a Pinocchio, made of wood and then turned into a real boy or girl. Adoption is a legal fiction, and Geppetto, the toymaker, could never claim to be Pinocchio's real father once he became a real boy, even through adoption. God does not "pretend" that we are children of God, just because we go through baptism or make a profession of faith. Consequently, the answer to our question is that we can never *become* an adopted child of God, because we *already are* a child of God.

---

101 Luke 15:11-32

CHAPTER 7

# End Times

## John of Patmos

Toward the end of the first century C.E. a man named John on the island of Patmos wrote the most controversial book in the New Testament, *Revelation*. The book also has the Greek name *Apocalypse*; both names mean a revealing or unveiling. As the Greek name indicates, Revelation belongs to the genre of apocalyptic literature. There were many similar books in the first several centuries that were widely read but eventually rejected. Revelation might not have made it into the canon had it not been for the belief that its author was John the apostle.

There are three authors of New Testament books ascribed to someone named John: the Gospel according to John, the three epistles of John and Revelation. The Greek literary style of the three authors is so vastly different that modern Scripture authorities agree that they were different persons. Since the Acts of the Apostles describes the apostle John as uneducated or illiterate,[102] the idea that he could write anything, especially in sophisticated Greek, is untenable. The author of the Gospel with his name, like the other evangelists, is anonymous. Likewise the author of the epistles of John is unknown, naming himself only as "the elder." In Revelation, however, the author identifies himself as John.

---

102 Acts 4:13

Until recently everyone thought John was a Gentile Christian. Behind this was the assumption that all who acclaimed Jesus as Messiah in the first century, especially New Testament authors, believed and taught exactly the same thing. Scripture scholars consistently interpreted the message of Revelation to fit Christian doctrines.

There are problems with such an assumption. One is that John of Patmos vehemently condemned the eating of food offered to idols, whereas the apostle Paul allowed it. Another is that John uses the term "church" as well as "synagogue;" and we have no reason to think that he either did not know the difference or used these words interchangeably. Furthermore, John is extremely familiar with the imagery of Isaiah, Jeremiah, Ezekiel and Daniel, and his contrasting the city of Rome with the heavenly Jerusalem does not fit the mentality of Gentile Christians, who were becoming more and more anti-Jewish and thought of Jerusalem only in terms of its destruction as punishment for the rejection of the Messiah. An example of the growing anti-Jewish sentiment is the Gospel of John, in which Jews are always adversaries of Jesus.

Elsewhere in the New Testament Christians are exhorted to obey civil law and pray for those in authority. For John, this attitude is unthinkable.

Consequently, the view gaining ground today is that John of Patmos accepted Jesus as the Messiah, but was also a devout Jew. He was not a Gentile convert to a new religion called Christianity, but a Jew who practiced Judaism just like every other Jew, except that he believed Jesus was the Jewish Messiah. It is possible, then, that he continued in the tradition of James, the brother of Jesus, and he might have belonged to the Jewish community that was later called the Ebionites.[103]

## The Letters to the Seven Churches

In the first chapters of Revelation, John addresses seven churches in Asia Minor, now present-day Turkey. The challenges facing these com-

---

103 John condemned eating food sacrificed to idols, which was usually meat, but said nothing about not eating meat altogether. If he was a member of the group that came to be the Ebionites, then the Ebionites had not yet adopted vegetarianism.

munities were persecution, participation in pagan worship and culture, and apathy. John warns the churches that they needed to reform, but he stresses even more a promise of hope and encouragement. To comprehend John's message, we ask what it meant to the seven churches, in their time, and when written by a Jewish follower of Jesus. Only then can we apply its lessons to ourselves.

Revelation has many bizarre images of evil and destruction. Hence, "apocalyptic" now implies the worst catastrophe. Our question here is, *what does the book of Revelation teach us about end times?*

## Plagues and Punishment

After John addresses the seven churches in chapters one to three, he begins to describe his vision. It may have been a real vision, possibly induced by prayer and fasting, or a creation of his own; but it still reflects the mentality of his own time and culture.

We see a typically Hebrew world view in chapter four as the vision unfolds. John looks up to heaven and sees an open door. The images in John's vision can be likened to a series of political cartoons. Throughout the book, John uses images familiar to his readers, in much the same way as we would use an eagle to represent America or a bear to stand for Russia. Sometimes he adds specific details to make sure his readers get the point, as when he refers to the seven hills, a clear designation of Rome. Other images could be considered exaggerations to stress his point. Today similar exaggerations are not only in political cartoons, but in other venues, like late night comedy television.

Chapters four to eleven can be read as a unit, which begins the vision with heavenly worship. Four living creatures, representing all living beings, sing "Holy, holy, holy…" Throughout the book the narrative is repeatedly interrupted by joyful hymns of praise. Then we have the scroll with seven seals. Only the Lion of the tribe of Judah is found worthy to open the seals, but the Lion turns out to be the Lamb, and immediately there is a hymn to the Lamb, used throughout the book as a symbol of Christ.

As six of the seals are broken open, disasters and punishments are poured out on earth one after another. After the sixth seal, there is a vision of 144,000 from Israel, 12,000 from each tribe. This scene inspired the line, "I want to be in that number," which is found in "When the Saints Go Marching In." The number is symbolic, since we also have a multitude *from every nation*. A heavenly hymn is sung, "Salvation belongs to our God..." The multitudes of Jews and Gentiles represent the saved.

In chapter 8 the Lamb opens the seventh seal. Seven angels with seven trumpets appear, and the plagues and destruction begin all over again. But after the sixth angel releases more of God's wrath, a seventh angel appears with a small scroll and tells John to eat it. He is then given the command to "prophesy again."

Eating the scroll is understood as John's mimicking the action of Ezekiel. In the third chapter of Ezekiel, the prophet is told to eat a scroll and then to preach what was written on the scroll. Ezekiel is the key to knowing what is going on with John when he eats the small scroll.

To put the scroll in context, we look at Revelation 9:20-21. Here we find the purpose of all the plagues and punishments. The rest of humanity that were still alive had not repented. They continued in their sinful acts and had failed to change. The purpose of all the destruction, then, was to get sinners to repent. But it had not worked. All the plagues and disasters had been useless. And so the angel tells John *not to write down* what he had witnessed. Instead, he is given a new scroll, told to eat it, and to prophesy again. *The punishments John had witnessed were undone, and John had a new message.*

Chapter eleven centers on the temple. John is told to measure the temple, and what follows sounds more like a description of the past destruction of the temple in the year 70 than a prediction of what is to come. Two witnesses then prophesy, and the beast from the bottomless pit kills them. After three and a half days the breath of life returns to them and they return to heaven. A tenth of the city (Jerusalem) or seven thousand people are killed in a great earthquake, and the rest give glory to God. The figures in this part of the vision — the beast, the two witnesses, the tenth of the city — are probably symbolic and do not refer to specific or historic details.

This section of Revelation is closed with the blowing of the seventh trumpet. Instead of more destruction, there is a hymn to the Messiah, and, from the twenty-four elders, a hymn to God. Then God's temple, already destroyed on earth, is opened in heaven, and the ark of God's covenant is seen. John would have seen the ark as a sign that the covenant with Abraham and Moses was still in effect. He would probably not have ascribed to the Gentile Christian theology of a new covenant, and placing the ark in the vision is another reason to see him as Jewish.

## Evil Is Overcome

Beginning in chapter twelve we leave behind the almost unending series of catastrophes and concentrate on the battle between specific symbolic figures. This section of Revelation, chapters twelve to twenty, begins with a great portent in heaven. A woman is clothed with the sun, with the moon under her feet, and with a crown of twelve stars. She is in agony, giving birth.

A great red dragon is ready to devour the woman's child as soon as it is born. She gives birth to a male child, who is to rule all nations with a rod of iron. After the child is snatched away and taken to God, the woman flees into the wilderness. Michael defeats the dragon, and there is a hymn. The dragon fights on earth and pursues the woman. As she flees, the dragon pours water like a river after her, but the earth itself saves her by swallowing the water. The dragon then turns to make war on the rest of the woman's children.

Who is the woman? Because her son is the Messiah, or Jesus, Catholic theologians have argued that she is Mary. The description of the woman is the way Mary appears in Catholic statues and pictures. However, the story does not fit Mary, especially in trying to explain who the rest of the woman's children are and her flight into the wilderness. The Catholic Church has consistently tried to avoid admitting that Mary had other children. Catholic theologians get around this by proposing that Mary is the spiritual mother of all Christians.

A second Catholic explanation is that the woman is the Church. The rest of the children would be Christians. However, it is not logical to see the Church as giving birth to the Messiah, since, in Christian theology, Jesus is supposed to be the founder of the Church, and the Church is typically the bride of Christ, not his mother.

The simplest explanation is that the woman is Israel or the Jewish nation. After the resurrection, or after the child is snatched up into heaven, the dragon pursues the rest of the woman's children, who would be the Jews, especially those who suffered in the destruction of Jerusalem and followed Jesus.

This explanation also makes sense with the author's style. John uses parallel images when he describes two cities, Rome and Jerusalem. We can expect to find the same use of parallel images when it comes to the two women in Revelation. The harlot is the Roman Empire. The opposing image is that of the woman clothed in the sun. If the harlot is a nation, then the woman giving birth to the Messiah would also be a nation, which would be Israel.

The dragon gives power to a beast, which makes war on the saints and conquers them. The beast is often referred to as the antichrist. However, the word "antichrist" is not used anywhere in the book of Revelation. A second beast decrees that everyone must be marked on the forehead or right hand in order to buy or sell. The number of the beast is six hundred sixty-six.

The mark of the beast is symbolic, but most scholars today believe that six hundred sixty-six signifies Nero. The reason for this is the use of gematria, or the symbolism of numbers. In the Greek and Hebrew alphabets, each letter stood for a number, since, without the invention of Arabic numerals, letters were the only symbols available to represent numbers. Thus the first letter of the alphabet stood for one, the second for two, and so on. The letters in everyone's name could be added up, and everyone knew what one's own number was and what anyone's name equaled. Six hundred sixty-six was the number for Nero Caesar in the Hebrew alphabet, and every Jew would have known this.

Gematria, or numeric symbolism, was important throughout Jewish history and in early Christian times. By the time the apostle Paul began writing, within a little more than fifteen years after the crucifixion, Paul had available a new, commonly recognized Greek name for the Messiah. Mary's son had an Aramaic name, Yeshua, which was not transliterated (or translated letter by letter) into Greek. If it had been so transliterated, we would today be calling Jesus Yeshua or maybe Joshua. Instead, the Greek name turned out to be *Iesous,* an artificially coined name that originated only with the preaching of the gospel to Greek-speaking Gentiles. It had to be a deliberate creation, and it is no coincidence that the number of *Iesous* adds up to eight hundred eighty-eight, a perfect number.

In chapter fourteen the Lamb appears on Mount Zion, which is where the temple was built. With the Lamb are 144,000 who had the name of the Lamb and of his Father on their foreheads. This is another parallel contrast with those who had the mark of the beast. The 144,000 sing a new song that only they could learn to sing. John describes them as virgins, not defiled with women. This may mean that they are like Israelite soldiers who lived apart from their wives in preparation for battle.

There are three angels. The first has an eternal gospel to proclaim to all on earth. The second proclaims the fall of Babylon, or Rome. The third proclaims that those who worship the beast with the mark on the forehead or hand will be tormented with no rest day or night. This is a call for the saints to endure.

One like a Son of Man is seated on a cloud. One angel with a sickle reaps the harvest of the earth. A second angel with a sickle gathers the vintage and throws it into the wine press of the wrath of God.

In chapter fifteen there is another portent, seven angels with seven plagues, and they sing a hymn. In chapter sixteen a voice from heaven commands the seven angels to pour out the seven bowls of God's wrath. After the third angel, there is a hymn proclaiming God's just judgment. Then the final four angels pour out their four bowls. In 16:16 the kings of the earth are assembled at Armageddon for battle. This is the only mention of this name in Revelation. *No battle at Armageddon* is mentioned.

## False Questions

In chapter seventeen one of the seven angels shows John the great harlot clothed in gold and jewels. On her forehead is "Babylon the Great," the great city that rules over the kings of the earth. This is the city or empire of Rome, which will be made desolate and burn with fire.

Then, in chapter eighteen, another angel proclaims that Babylon has fallen. All those who depend on Rome for their wealth, such as merchants, are in mourning. We can see here the uselessness in being marked with the sign of the beast, which was needed to buy or sell; it also demonstrates the punishment for accepting this seal. Further, we see the mark of the beast as something taking place *in John's own time* and not as something to happen in the far distant future.

Chapter nineteen has a hymn of rejoicing in heaven: "Blessed are those who are invited to the marriage supper of the Lamb." Heaven opens, and there is a rider on a white horse, whose name is The Word of God, the King of kings and Lord of lords. From his mouth comes a sharp sword to strike down the nations. The armies of the earth make war against the rider. The armies, with the beast and the false prophet, are conquered. There is no mention of armies of saints or followers of the Lamb. *The only weapon is the sword of truth* in the mouth of the Lamb. Hence the most effective weapon against evil is truth.

John emphasized the traditional Jewish image of the Messiah as one who would conquer the nations *in behalf of Israel*.

Finally, in chapter twenty, an angel seizes the dragon, the ancient serpent who is the Devil and Satan, and throws him into the pit and seals it for a thousand years. After the thousand years Satan is released, and he gathers the nations for battle. They surround the camp of the saints and beloved city, but are thrown into the lake of fire. Judgment comes to all according to their works. Those whose names are not in the book of life are thrown into the lake of fire.

The saints are associated with the "beloved city," which is Jerusalem. John identifies the saints, or believers in Jesus, with *Jewish* believers.

## The Heavenly Jerusalem

The final section of Revelation comprises chapters twenty-one and twenty-two. This is the vision of a new heaven and a new earth, or a new heaven *on* earth. The holy city, the new Jerusalem, comes down from heaven as a bride adorned for her husband. Then there is hymn: Death will be no more. The new Jerusalem is not built from below as an earthly city, such as Rome, but comes from above.

One of the seven angels shows John the bride, the wife of the Lamb, which is the new Jerusalem. In the Old Testament, Israel was pictured as God's bride. Gentile Christianity pictured the Church as the bride of Christ, but here the bride is not the Gentile Christian Church, but the city of Jerusalem, or the Jewish people.

Popular imagery has St. Peter letting people into heaven through one set of pearly gates. This is not the limited vision of John. The new Jerusalem has high walls with twelve gates with names of the twelve tribes inscribed, and twelve foundations with names of the twelve apostles of the Lamb. Its gates will *never be shut*.

The city measures 1500 miles long, 1500 miles wide and 1500 miles high. It would have swallowed up the Roman Empire. It has walls of jasper and is a city of pure gold. The twelve gates are twelve pearls.

There is no temple in the city, because the temple is God and the Lamb. There is no need for sun or moon, and there is no night. And the nations will walk by its light.

Flowing from the throne of God through the city is the river of the water of life. The message, intended especially for the seven churches, is, "Take heed, I am coming soon; my reward is with me, to repay all according to their deeds."[104] There is a hymn: "The spirit and the bride say, 'Come.' And let whoever hears, say, 'Come.' And let whoever is thirsty, come. Let whoever has the desire, take the water of life for free."[105]

---

104 Revelation 22:12
105 Revelation 22:17

*False Questions*

The book of Revelation ends with a universal message of hope, both for the followers of Jesus and the nations. We note the following: The author was evidently a Jewish follower of Jesus and someone who rejected Paul's concessions to Gentile converts. Jesus was the Jewish Messiah, and salvation comes through Jesus but also through Israel. The traditional Old Testament image of the Messiah as the glorious conqueror is restored. Jesus is described as the Lion, the Lamb, and God's son, but there is no mention of the Holy Spirit or of a Trinity. Jesus is exalted, but not made equal to God or made divine. The bride of Christ is not the Church, but the new Jerusalem.

Further, the book is not a map of future events. Instead, John expected his prophecy to be fulfilled "soon." Rome was built on evil practices under the influence of the devil, and John expected those evil practices to bring about its immediate downfall. This, of course, did not happen. Even so, Revelation conveys an overriding and compelling message of hope.

Although there are catastrophes described in Revelation, they are interspersed with hymns of hope and praise. The book does not end in disaster, but in the victory of God and the Lamb. Israel gives birth to the child, who destroys the harlot Rome. The new Jerusalem descends from heaven, and all nations are saved through the nation of Israel and her Messiah, the Lamb.

## Our Answer

The events portrayed in Revelation are symbolic, and John of Patmos expected them to happen *soon*, not in future centuries. *What, then, does the book of Revelation teach us about end times?* The answer: *Revelation teaches us nothing about end times.* Nor does it mention an antichrist or a battle at Armageddon. Revelation is the most misunderstood book of the New Testament.

## Lessons from the Book of Revelation

The book of Revelation stands in continuity with other books in the New Testament through its vision of the immediate return of Jesus.

Together with John the Baptist, Jesus and the apostle Paul, John of Patmos expects the immediate triumph of good over evil "soon." And like the other three, he was wrong. Christianity eventually conquered the Roman Empire when Constantine came to power, but its victory was hardly the dramatic and catastrophic conquest described in John's vision.

Of the two visions and their opposing messages, that of Paul and that of John of Patmos, the former became the one adopted by Christian churches, while the latter is more in agreement with what Jesus preached. John was, like Jesus and his brother, James the Just, also a faithful Jew. History, however, was written by the winners, who were the Gentile Christians and not the Jewish followers of Jesus.

On the other hand, a fresh reading of Revelation uncovers a *contrasting but equally valid view* of who Jesus is and what he taught. For John, those washed in the blood of the Lamb are the *Jewish* followers, and the Lamb conquers the evil rampant among the Gentiles by the *sword of truth* that comes from his mouth. Completely out of mind is the theological view of Paul, who preached the vicarious redemption of all humankind independent of the people of Israel.

John of Patmos reminds us of the need to concentrate on *the sword of truth,* the message which Jesus delivered to the Galileans. Christians have had endless and ugly debates on *who* Jesus is. The sword of truth reminds us to *heed what he taught.*

CHAPTER 8

# Our Spiritual Path

On our spiritual journey we must walk on solid ground, with fundamental truths to guide us. We may revise our beliefs later on, but we can start with our own convictions.

I suggest that you begin by writing your own creed. I have created a sample creed or profession of faith based primarily upon the Gospels:

| | |
|---|---|
| I believe that God is our Father (and Mother). | (Matthew 6:9) |
| We are all God's children. | (1 John 3:2) |
| God is love. | (1 John 4:8) |
| God always forgives | (Luke 7:36-50) |
| We must forgive others. | (Matthew 18:23-35) |
| We must love our enemies. | (Matthew 5:43-48) |
| True religion is to provide for those in need. | (James 1:27) |

You can at any time remove items from your creed or add new statements. You can add what you believe from your own personal experiences, such as near-death experiences, out-of-body experiences, after-death communications, dreams, meditations or other events and insights. Your spiritual journey is your own and must be built on what you experience and not just on what others tell you. Learn to trust yourself.

In the next few sections I will offer some spiritual practices based on Jesus' teachings. They are simple to use and can be modified to suit your own preferences, nor do they require changing your daily schedule.

## A. Seeing

The spiritual practice of *Seeing* is based on the way Jesus taught us to address God as Father, especially in the Lord's Prayer. Nowhere in the Gospels do we find Jesus calling God anything other than Father — not Creator, nor Father Almighty (as in the Apostles' Creed), nor by any of the names used in the Hebrew Scriptures. "Father" is the only way Jesus taught his followers to address God.

If God is Father to us, then we are God's children. Our relationship with our Father is described in the parable of the prodigal son. The prodigal may be said to be born again, but in the sense that his conversion or rebirth takes place when he remembers who he is — who he always was and always will be — the son of his father.

The practice of *Seeing* is a means to increase your spiritual vision by seeing yourself and others as God sees you. It can be part of your daily prayers, but I suggest that you make it a habit at other times of the day. When you are shopping, exercising in the gym, watching the news on television or catching a glimpse of a beggar on the street, remind yourself that they are God's children. Remember that they and you are children of the same Father, and therefore you are all sisters and brothers. It may help to visualize them as spiritual beings of light.

This practice does not require that you agree with my explanation of how we are God's children. You can practice *Seeing* in your own way, and you can begin with a prayer asking for help to see others as God sees them. Acknowledge that in God's eyes everyone is lovable. Do not be discouraged if you find it difficult to see some, maybe criminals or tyrants or someone who has abused you, as children of God. Just pray for help in seeing in them the divine spark or whatever makes them worth loving.

*Seeing* is a practice of reminding ourselves that we are all lovable, and that God loves everyone. As a spiritual *practice*, it is something we must repeat over and over for it to make it habitual. We cannot do it well or easily unless we do it consistently.

## B. Forgiving

The spiritual practice of *Forgiving* is, like *Seeing*, based on the Lord's Prayer, "Forgive us our trespasses as we forgive those who trespass against us." There are two other passages that are fundamental to this practice: 1) Matthew 18:21-35, the parable of the unjust servant (steward) and 2) Luke 7:36-50, the story of the woman who anointed Jesus' feet.

From these three sources we conclude that 1) God always forgives. 2) The only way to block the benefit of God's forgiveness is to refuse to forgive others. 3) Therefore we must forgive everyone who offends or hurts us, and we must do so over and over again.

We are not *reservoirs* of God's love and forgiveness. We are *channels*.

*Forgiving* is not a one-time action, but a *practice* to be repeated constantly. Some find this practice difficult, so here are some suggestions to make it easier:

*First*, learn to forgive yourself. God always forgives you, even before you ask. Learn to acknowledge the gift, not just with regret, but with love and gratitude, and by forgiving others.

*Second*, do not confuse forgiving with suffering abuse. If you are in an abusive situation, get out of it as soon as you can. Never let yourself become a victim of any kind of abuse — verbal, mental or physical. To do so is not a virtue and never helps you or anyone else.

*Third*, you may find it hard to forgive certain people or offenses. If so, admit the difficulty, but do not think that something is wrong with you. Change the way you approach this practice.

It is often the small things that hinder us from growing spiritually and not the big things. If you want to run a marathon, you don't start by running twenty-five miles the first day. First you run around the block, then you run a mile, then five miles, and you keep on running farther and farther. Forgiveness takes practice; learn by starting off small but be consistent. Start working on forgiving small slights and offenses, such as when people ignore you, cut you off in traffic or step in front of you in the grocery line. Practice in forgiving small things makes it easier to forgive big things.

When you leave this life, you leave everything behind, except for one thing, your relationships. When someone hurts you, whether in a big way or a small way, that relationship is damaged; and it is like both of you being chained to each other. This chain does not automatically go away over time. Anger and resentment will only make the chain heavier and more painful. But you have the power to forgive, and when you use the power to forgive, you break the chain, and both of you are free.

When *Forgiving* is difficult, be sure that you are still practicing *Seeing*. Unless you can see that those you need to forgive are lovable in God's eyes — unless you can see that God can also forgive your enemies — you will find *Forgiving* impossible. To forgive is to love, and you cannot love someone unless you see that person as lovable.

Don't worry about being forgiven. You have already received forgiveness in abundance. Forgiveness is not the gift you need to *receive*. It is *the gift you need to give*.

## C. Blessing

The practice of *Blessing* is often forgotten. As Christianity took shape, the new hierarchy of bishops and priests assumed for themselves alone spiritual power and authority, including the power to bless. In today's world Christians never dream of giving a blessing, except for a prayer before meals. Even then, if a minister or priest is present, the lay person defers to the clergy.

You cannot begin the practice of *Blessing* unless you believe you have the power to bless. Do you have this power and how does it work?

Genesis 27 provides an example of a blessing in the story of Isaac, who had twin sons, Esau and Jacob. Since Esau was the older, Isaac intended to pass on to him the blessing of becoming the father of God's chosen people. As Isaac lay dying, Jacob pretended to be Esau and tricked his father into giving him the blessing that Isaac intended to give to his brother. When Esau came into his father Isaac's tent and asked for the blessing, Isaac was dismayed. He had been deceived into making Jacob the father of God's chosen people. Esau was too late, and he had to settle for a lesser blessing instead.

When Isaac realized that he had given his blessing to the wrong son, why didn't he just say, "Oh, I made a mistake. I'll just take that blessing back and give it to you, Esau," instead?

The reason is that the Hebrews believed that our spoken word, once pronounced, continued on. The spoken word had its own existence, and there was no way to take it back. A word, once spoken had a life of its own. Its power continued on, so that the power of the word always continued to produce its effect. So if you can speak, you can bless.

We see a similar idea elsewhere in the Bible. God says, "Let there be light," and there was light. God's spoken word had the power to create whatever the word meant. In other words, our power to speak is a way in which we share God's power to create.

The biblical idea of a blessing is based on the irreversible power of the spoken word. It is more than a prayer. We say what we *intend* to happen, and speaking our intention *makes* it happen. Blessings are very real.

But so are curses. Our words and our intentions have real effects. That is why Jesus tell us to bless not only those who hate us, but those who curse us.[106]

In giving a blessing, we often use more than words to express a firm intention. We have the laying on of hands. We use the sign of the cross. We sprinkle with holy water. We anoint with oil. Or we may encircle a sick person and join hands. All these are ways that we often use, either with or without words, to express our *firm intention* that something good happen.

We give blessings so that someone may receive God's love, God's strength, God's peace or consolation, or some kind of divine healing, either physical or spiritual. We bless people and we bless things. We bless food and crops. We bless cars and homes, to ask for God's protection. A blessing is a spiritual action, so that it is intended to connect one with the divine. Whoever receives a blessing is supposed to be made holier or brought closer to God in some way, and that is the essential effect of a blessing. A sick person may not get well, crops may still wither, and the blessing of a car may not work over ninety miles an hour. But when someone is blessed, that person should be brought closer to God. Otherwise a blessing has no meaning.

Who can bless, and where does the power to bless come from? Jesus command us: "Bless those who curse you. Pray for those who harm you."[107] We cannot obey his command unless we have the power to bless. The power of *Blessing* is one you already have; you don't get it from the apostles, since they designated no one to succeed them. It is not restricted to a privileged few, since Jesus expected *everyone* to bless their enemies. The power to bless is innate in every child of God.

If you are in a group and find that someone is ailing, invite the group to join in a blessing for the sick person.

---

106 Luke 6:28
107 Ibid.

*False Questions*

---

You cannot bless someone without sincerely intending good for that person. How sincere you are depends upon the love you have. Consequently, love is the power behind every blessing — the power that determines how effective it will be.

Your ability to practice *Blessing* requires that you *see* others as lovable and can love and *forgive* them. You have the power of love to bring God's blessing and love into the world. You do not need ordination. You need no commission or authorization. Instead, you have the *command* of Jesus to bless your enemies. See this as a huge opportunity — your chance to use God's love and power to change the world. Christ came to bring the blessing of peace on earth. When it comes, it will come through you and others like you.

You can practice *Blessing* in your daily prayers or at any time in the day. All you need is a sincere intention. But it is a practice that requires repetition. Like any prayer, its effectiveness is increased by doing it with others.

## D. Giving Thanks

If we see ourselves as God's children and acknowledge the gift of God's forgiveness, then the practice of *Giving Thanks* should come naturally. In the Gospels Jesus gives thanks to his Father, and we see that he expects this attitude from his followers:

> [11]On the way to Jerusalem, Jesus passed through the territory between Samaria and Galilee. [12]As he was entering a village, ten men who were lepers came up to meet him. They stood some distance back and [13]cried out, "Jesus, Master, have mercy on us!" [14]When he saw them, he said, "Go, and show yourselves to the priests." And as they were going on their way, they were made clean of their leprosy. [15]One of them, seeing that he was healed, went back to Jesus, shouting God's praises. [16]He threw himself down, with his face at Jesus' feet, and thanked him. And he was a Samaritan.
>
> [17]Jesus replied, "Weren't there ten who were made clean? Where are the other nine? [18]No one returns and gives praise to God except this foreigner?" [19]And he said to him, "Stand up and be on your way. Your faith [faithfulness or steadfastness] has saved you."[108]

One reason Christians allege for going to church is to worship or praise God. In some churches the worship service is called the Eucharist, which means thanksgiving. Whether or not God needs or wants worship, praise or even thanks, *we* need to be thankful. Mothers and fathers do more for their children than their children will ever know, and they love and care for their children whether they receive thanks or not. Parents always appreciate being thanked, but they teach their children to be grateful and say "Thank you" not so much because they have to receive gratitude, but because their children need to be grateful. In the same way, God may not need our gratitude, but to grow spiritually we need to be grateful.

---

108 Luke 17:11-19

*False Questions*

Like the other three practices, *Giving Thanks* has to be a regularly repeated practice. It can be done at any time, but to make it a permanent way of thinking, it is good to do it on a regular schedule, such as after meals or together with other prayers or meditation.

At the same time, thanking God for all we have and are, even if done every day, requires another essential ingredient, which is to express our gratitude to others. Besides saying "Thank you" or sending "Thank you" notes, we need to be generous in returning acts of kindness.

Everyone experiences tragedies and evil at various times and to varying degrees. It is hard at these times to be grateful, but it becomes easier if we have made it a practice of *Giving Thanks* frequently for the *small gifts* of life. Like *Forgiving*, we find it easier to face the big challenges if we practice *Giving Thanks* for small things.

There are certainly other practices that help us grow spiritually. The four explained here, though, are fundamental. They are most beneficial if they are all practiced consistently and together. To do so is an expression of our steadfastness or faithfulness, which in the Gospels is expressed by the word "faith."

APPENDIX A

# Mistranslated Words

Words constantly change in meaning in every spoken language. In English, for example, the word "guy" in the 1970s always meant a male. By the twenty-first century usage had changed, so that the plural of this word could also refer to females. Similarly, the words "pot" and "weed" in the 2000s are frequently used for marijuana, but in the 1800s they would never have been understood in this sense.

It is easy to read into biblical terms our own definitions. When we use a word such as "faith" every day with a common definition, we naturally give it the same meaning in a biblical context, without realizing that the word had a different meaning in the first century C.E.

Most of the vocabulary in a modern translation of the Bible is, of course, to be understood as we understand the rest of the English language. But this is not always true. The only way to be sure that the words in your version of the Bible mean what you think they mean, is to use a complete biblical concordance, which for each word gives the original Hebrew or Greek word, what it meant in the time it was written, and where it is found in the Bible.

The following are some commonly misunderstood words found in the Bible:

BISHOP/PRIEST/DEACON: Even Eusebius in the fourth century made the mistake of reading his own technical definitions of these words into the

*False Questions*

New Testament and ecclesiastical history. Throughout the first century *episkopos* (bishop) meant overseer, *presbyter* (priest) meant elder and *diakonos* (deacon) meant servant. The ecclesiastical offices we assign to these words did not exist until the second century.

CHURCH: Used to translate the Greek *ekklesía*, this word means a group or community called together. *Young's Analytical Concordance to the Bible* defines it as "that which is called out." It never means an organized religion.

DEATH AND SIN: Although these words often have the same meaning we give them today, Paul also used the words to designate cosmic power. So when Paul, like others in his time, says that Jesus conquered sin and death, he is usually thinking of cosmic powers holding sway over humanity.

FAITH: Sometime in the second century this word began to be used for belief in a set of doctrines. Except for the Pastoral Epistles, which were composed by someone other than Paul at least as late as the end of the first century, *faith* is never used in the New Testament in this way. Instead, it denotes faithfulness, steadfastness or fidelity. When it connotes belief, it is belief or trust in another person, not in teachings or dogmas.

FEET: In the third chapter of Ruth is an example of a euphemism. Feet in Hebrew often referred to genitals. Translators seem to avoid euphemisms, preferring literal translations instead.

GOLD RINGS: James 2:2 is an example not of a translation but of historical context. In reading this verse, be aware that the primary wearers of gold rings were those on a par with Roman senators. Was the author warning that Christians should avoid playing politics?

GRACE: This word is best translated as "favor." It never means a "thing," such as actual and sanctifying grace, which are theological ideas created centuries after the Bible was written. We might also substitute the word *kindness* in place of *grace*.

HOLY SPIRIT: Translators mislead the reader by capitalizing these words. In so doing, they are not just translating, but adding a theological interpretation implying that the authors believed the holy spirit was a separate divine person. This belief was not crystallized until centuries later. The Greek word for spirit is *pneuma,* whose basic meaning is breath or wind. (The Hebrew word for spirit had identical meanings.) As extended meanings, the Greek word could also be used to designate life or power. Consequently, when we read the Greek New Testament and come across "holy spirit," this can just as easily be translated as "sacred power" or "holy wind." These words often indicate divine action, but not on the part of a *separate* divine entity.

To understand how the Jews of Jesus' time used the word "spirit," we look at their Old Testament scriptures. The Hebrew word for spirit was *ruah,* which meant spirit, breath and wind — and all at the same time. The *ruah* or spirit of God was God's breath. Thus God breathed the breath of life into the first humans, thereby giving them God's spirit. When we die we stop breathing, which means giving up our spirit. The wind was pictured as God's breath, as though God were breathing hard or violently.

The same ideas are at work in the New Testament. At Pentecost there was a "violent wind,"[109] and wind and spirit would have been the same in the Hebrew mind. In John 3:8 we read, "The wind blows where it chooses," and a footnote in the New Revised Standard Version tells us, "The same Greek word means both *wind* and *spirit.*"

Instead of reading *into* the New Testament the dogma of the Holy Spirit, we would do better to understand that *holy spirit* is a continuation

---

109 Acts 2:2

of the same Old Testament or Hebrew notion of *spirit (breath, wind) of God*.

In Genesis 1:2, *ruah* is variously translated as the "spirit" of God over the waters or as a "wind" from God blowing over the waters. This use of the word *ruah* in the Hebrew is parallel to how the word *pneuma* was used in the Greek, so that "holy spirit" simply meant the "spirit of God," or the activity or presence of God. The personification of the words "holy spirit," or making the words refer to a distinct divine person, is an understanding that happened after the New Testament was written.

KINGDOM OF GOD: Many translators prefer "reign of God" rather than "kingdom of God." The reason is that kingdom connotes a territory or place, whereas the Greek term *basileia* indicates a condition or state of being. Thus to enter the kingdom of God does not mean going to the Holy Land or to heaven, but submitting to God's rule. The kingdom of God designated a state of total renewal to take place here on earth.

DOUBLE MEANINGS: 1 Peter 3:21-22 offers the only New Testament definition of baptism. In this pericope the *New Revised Standard Version* says baptism is "an appeal to God for a good conscience." However, a footnote indicates that the same Greek words could be translated as "a pledge to God for a good conscience." Always read footnotes to learn problems in translations, such as double meanings. In this instance I believe that both meanings were intended by the author.

APPENDIX B

# How to Interpret the Bible

The basic book for Christians is the Bible, which has as many interpretations as there are readers. Guidelines are a must for all readers, including biblical scholars.

A hundred or so years ago most English speaking Christians read only one of two English biblical translations: 1) The King James version among Protestants, and 2) The Douay version for Catholics. Today there are multiple versions translated from the original languages and making use of the most recent findings from ancient texts, such as the Dead Sea Scrolls, and archeology. Translators, though, have their limitations. They cannot completely convey the differences in authors' styles. They are puzzled over how to translate words with double meanings. They are faced with variant readings without a way to determine which is preferable.

I suggest that you use two or more recent English versions side by side. Add to these a book called a concordance, which lists in alphabetical order every word in the Bible, along with the book, chapter and verse where it is found, a portion of the sentence in which it occurs, and the meaning of the word in the original language.

Scripture scholars have long tried to create a standardized Hebrew and Greek text of the Bible. Translators use these various standardized texts, and while they far surpass what was used for the first English translations, there is no common standardized text that agrees with any one ancient document. Become aware of this problem by consulting commentaries and reading footnotes found in some English Bibles.

The primary question for every reader is, what did the author mean? or how did the author's first audience understand the text? It is essential to interpret the Bible in its literary and historical context.

A second question for the reader must be, what kind of literature is the author writing? Different forms of literature are meant to be read in different ways. For example, pick up a newspaper. What you find on the front page you can read as factual, or at least as someone's view of the facts. This is not true of the editorial page, where you may find some facts, but scattered along with a huge dose of personal opinion. Then glance at the advertisements; some are presented as factual, but can be mostly creative fiction. Likewise, the social column, the personal advice column, the comic strips, the feature articles, the obituaries — all require a different perspective by which to interpret them properly.

The Bible, too, contains a variety of literary forms. It is a mistake to read all the narrative (i.e., non-poetic) sections as though they were modern history. Biblical writers had no concept of historical writing as we know it today. For them, history was packaged with myth and religion, so that numbers and factual details could be readily altered if it furthered the author's religious view of truth. Our modern histories, too, are written by winners who have their own subtle ways of distorting facts.

## Problems in the Bible

We must acknowledge problems and contradictions in the Bible. Consider Genesis 12, 20, and 26, where we find three accounts of a patriarch passing off his wife as his sister. The first is about Abraham, Sarah, and the pharaoh, the second about Abraham, Sarah, and Abimelech, and the third about Isaac, Rebekah, and Abimelech. Can all three be factual? We can credit the author (or editor) for preserving these stories without attempting to reconcile them, but does it make any difference which one is true? Does it matter if none is factual?

The New Testament details two versions of the death of Judas. In Matthew 27:5 he hanged himself, whereas in Acts 1:18 he purchased land and died after a fall. Only one account can be true. Is either one true? Does it matter?

According to Matthew, Mark, and Luke, Jesus and his apostles celebrated the last supper on the eve of the Passover. John states Jesus was crucified on the day of the Passover. Matthew has Jesus dying around noon. John says he died late in the day. Which version is correct? Is one story based on faulty information? Or did one of the authors deliberately change the story? If so, why?

There are two versions of the beatitudes, differing in what Jesus said and where he said it. There are also two of the Lord's Prayer and two of the words of the last supper. If the authors of sacred scripture were to be courtroom witnesses, any judge would discount their conflicting testimony. However, these problems are not a basis for dismissal of the Bible as unreliable. Instead, we must approach our exegesis systematically to ascertain the reasons for the conflicts.

## Interpreting the Gospels

The Gospels deserve special attention because of what is called the "Synoptic problem." "Synoptic" means "from the same point of view," and we have three very similar Gospels written from a common perspective; these are Matthew, Mark, and Luke. These Gospels are not just similar; they are often word-for-word the same. At the same time, they often disagree in specific details, such as the order of events and even in the events themselves.

By laying out the Synoptic Gospels side by side, scholars have reached general agreement that Matthew and Luke copied from Mark. However, there is considerable material that is common to Matthew and Luke that is not found in Mark. That material is labeled "Q" to designate an unknown common source for these two Gospels. Material exclusive to each evangelist may come from each one's sources or may be each one's theological creation.

*False Questions*

The Gospel according to John both agrees and disagrees with the synoptic Gospels in many instances.

Concentrating especially on the Gospels, our rules for biblical interpretation include the following:

1) If we know which version of a Gospel is the older, then *the older version is usually to be preferred.* An example is in the last supper account. The first one written is by Paul in First Corinthians, and it predates the Gospel accounts, which are probably taken from liturgies currently in use.

2) If two authors relate an event *using independent sources,* the event is likely to be historical.

3) *The shorter of two readings is usually to be preferred.* Thus the beatitudes of Luke are probably closer to the original words of Jesus than the expanded version of Matthew. And Luke's version of the Lord's Prayer is closer to the original than Matthew's, which is the longer of the two. We presume that the evangelists would tend to preserve details or embellish their story rather than to delete them. Editors are more likely to add words (to explain the context) than to omit words.

As stories are retold, details are added more often than omitted. For example, in the passion narrative Mark says a bystander in the Garden of Olives cut off the ear of a slave of the high priest. Luke, writing later, adds that it was the right ear and that Jesus healed the man. By the time John writes, the one wielding the sword is Peter and the servant is Malchus. It is more likely that details were created in retelling the story than that Mark deliberately omitted them.

4) If one passage is easier to understand than the same passage in a different manuscript, version or Gospel, then *we usually prefer the reading that is more difficult.* The reason is that if a passage

is going to be changed, it is more likely to be changed to make it easier to understand than to make it more difficult.

5) Details contrary to an author's position are apt to be factual, because there would be no reason to invent them. Thus, since Jesus' baptism by John was a submissive act that embarrassed the early Church and was used by John's disciples against the Christians, it likely has a historical basis.

6) Sayings that do not fit well together are probably close to the original. They may have been joined to avoid losing them. On the other hand, if some verses seem to interrupt the flow of a passage, we can suspect that those verses may not have been part of the author's original work.

7) Items unusual or without precedent are apt to be genuine. Examples are Jesus' sayings with "Amen, amen, I say to you." Some might include here the description of him as an exorcist or his consistent invocation to God as "Father." (Not all experts agree, and this rule is open to personal interpretation.)

8) Artificial literary arrangements are the creation of the author. For instance, Mark makes the passion narrative fit Psalm 22. Matthew divided his Gospel into units composed of Jesus' sayings and deeds. That there are five such sections suggests a reflection of the Pentateuch, that is, the five books credited to Moses. Jesus' preaching from the mountain is an image of him as the new Moses or lawgiver. Another evident literary device is the frequent pattern in which the Pharisees question, Jesus questions, the Pharisees answer, and then Jesus gives the final answer. We can also include the long speeches of Jesus related by John.

9) We must always fit our documents into their historical context. If what we know for certain from other historical data contradicts what is in our biblical or other religious text, then we must con-

sider that portion of our text as not historical and the creation of the author. An example would be any of the mistaken geographical details as in Mark.

10) There are specific guidelines for dating works: a) Language and vocabulary may place a literary work in a specific period. b) Details of known historical events or customs indicate a current or subsequent date. c) If one author quotes another, the first must postdate the latter; but at times we cannot discount two authors using another common source. d) Carbon dating can at times place a document in a certain period, so that it would have to be written by that time. e) Paleography (the study of handwriting) can be used to determine a general time frame, once the dates of similarly written documents are known. It is not foolproof, and internal testimony, such as descriptions of events and vocabulary, must also be considered.

11) As we take up the individual Gospels, *we must not use one to interpret another.* Each evangelist wrote an individual book to stand on its own, as though it was the only Gospel to be written. We find that those who wrote later did not agree with what came before, but changed and contradicted those who wrote earlier.

APPENDIX C

# Matthew's Use of Isaiah 7:14

Matthew used Isaiah 7:14 to prove that Jesus fulfilled a prophecy of being born of a virgin. I am only addressing how Matthew used his sources, and not whether the virgin birth actually occurred, since this is a matter of faith rather than history.

*First*, the Greek Septuagint does translate Isaiah's word for maiden or young woman as "virgin." In a Greek-speaking world, Christians found the Septuagint to be a readily available translation. Whenever we find early Christian authors quoting the Hebrew Scriptures, they are most often using the Septuagint.

Matthew, too, must have been quoting the Septuagint. Since it uses the word "virgin," Matthew does likewise. This is what we would expect him to do.

*Second*, we ask how a translation can help to understand a manuscript in an author's native language. At times some have believed that certain translations were superior to the Bible in the original language. For example, some today still rely entirely on the King James Version. From the end of the sixteenth century into the twentieth, English-speaking Catholics read the Douay Bible, which was a translation not from Hebrew and Greek, but from the Latin Vulgate.

There are times when a translation may be useful. One example is when a Hebrew word is used only once or twice, so that we are unsure of its meaning. A Greek or Coptic translation may be helpful to understand what the author meant. Another case is when there are gaps or missing words in a manuscript. A complete manuscript in a different language may indicate what words in the original could be missing.

Sometimes, then, a translation may help to determine the meaning of a manuscript in the author's original language, especially when the meaning is in doubt. This is not the case here.

*Third*, we ask whether the Septuagint could be more reliable than the Hebrew version. Occasionally we do not know which of two or more copies in an original language may be correct, and we may be able to use a translation to find the answer. Until the discovery of the Qumran scrolls, our oldest Hebrew copies of the Old Testament were codices that dated to around the year 900. These are also known as the Masoretic text, which may have become the Jewish standard as early as the year 100. Until that time there were variant wordings of many Old Testament books.

Among the discoveries at Qumran were manuscripts of all the Old Testament books except Esther. Most of these affirm the accuracy of the Masoretic text, but one partial exception is Isaiah, the only complete book recovered. Isaiah is a version that was linguistically updated. As in all languages, words can change in meaning or may be replaced by other words. The Qumran version of Isaiah was updated or "modernized" to make it easier to read.

At times the Septuagint reflects an original Hebrew version that differs from the Masoretic text. The Qumran Isaiah is an example that shows that such divergent texts existed. When we have evidence that the translators of the Septuagint had a Hebrew text that we no longer have, we call that divergent, lost text a Vorlage.

In general, the Qumran scrolls confirm the accuracy of the Masoretic text. This is amazing, since there is about a thousand-year gap between these scrolls and the Masoretic codices. In comparison with the stability of the Masoretic text, the many ancient copies of New Testament books have more variations than the New Testament has words.

The question, then, is whether the Septuagint translation of Isaiah 7:14 could have depended upon a Vorlage more reliable than the Masoretic text. If so, the Qumran Isaiah is not the one. Although the

Qumran Isaiah diverges often from the Masoretic text, it retains the word *almah* or "young woman" in chapter seven, verse fourteen. The Septuagint translation of the Hebrew *almah* into the Greek *parthenos* or "virgin" likely resulted not from a Vorlage but from how the translators understood the word. It may be that the Egyptian Jews thought of any young woman of marriageable age to be a virgin, or that the Greek word "virgin" could also refer to any young woman. We cannot be certain.

The Qumran scrolls helped scholars to correct older translations; but without contrary evidence, they also confirm the reliability of the Masoretic text. The result is that new translations prefer the Masoretic text over the Septuagint, and use such words as "young woman" or "maiden" for Isaiah 7:14, while at times noting that the word "virgin" appears in the Greek text.

It is possible that Isaiah used a word that specifically meant virgin, but there is no textual evidence for this. Without any evidence, we cannot argue from what is *possible* to what is *actually* true. Consequently, there is no reason to prefer the Septuagint over the Masoretic text, either in general or for the translation of Isaiah 7:14.

*Fourth*, we need to examine the *context* of this verse in Isaiah 7:10-17:

> [10]Once more the Lord spoke to Ahaz, saying, [11]"Ask the Lord your God for a sign; let it be deep as the world below or as high as the heaven above." [12]But Ahaz said, "I will not ask, and I will not give the Lord a test."
>
> [13]Then Isaiah said: "Then hear, house of David! It is not enough for you to annoy humans, so that you have to annoy my God as well? [14]Consequently, the Lord himself will give you a sign. Behold, the young woman is (will be) with child and will bear a son, and she will give him the name of Immanuel. [15]By the time he is eating curds and honey, he will be able to turn away from evil and do what is good. [16] For before the child knows how to turn away from evil and do what is good, the land of the two kings you fear will be abandoned. [17]Through the king of Assyria, the Lord will bring on you and on your people and on your descendants days that

> have not been seen since the day that Ephraim separated from Judah."[110]

Earlier in chapter seven we read that King Rezin of Syria (Aram) and King Pekah of the Northern Kingdom of Israel had joined hands to attack King Ahaz and Jerusalem. Isaiah goes to advise Ahaz and tell him not to be afraid. Ahaz is told to ask God for a sign, presumably of his choosing, to show that he will be victorious; but he refuses, saying that he will not put God to a test. Isaiah rebukes him and says that God will give a sign anyway.

The word "behold" can also be translated as "look," "here," or "see." The person spoken to is supposed to be able to see the object of "behold." In this case, the one Ahaz is to behold is the young woman, *who had to be present*. It is not just "a" or "any" young woman, but the definite article is used, indicating *the* young woman *who was present*. The Hebrew noun used here is *almah*, which stresses the meaning of youth, without any connotation of virginity.

The most likely reading is that the young woman *is* with child. The present tense is indicated, so that the young woman is *already* pregnant. And if she is already pregnant, it would make no sense for Isaiah to call her a virgin. If — though less likely — we read that the young woman *will* be with child, then Isaiah could have used a word that implied virginity, but only virginity at the time Isaiah is speaking, not in the sense of a virgin birth.

The translation I have given reads, "she will give him the name of Immanuel." The preferable reading is probably "you will give him…," indicating that Isaiah is speaking directly to the young woman. In either case it is the *young woman who is present* who is going to name the child.

Immanuel means "God is with us." Because the child is to be a sign that Ahaz will prevail, the obvious meaning is that the birth of the child will signal the victory brought about because God was with Ahaz and his

---

110 Isaiah 7:10-17

people. The final victory will happen when the child grows up and learns the difference between good and evil, that is, when he reaches the use of reason or the age of maturity.

Isaiah's prediction is the fall from power of the two kings threatening Ahaz, and that prediction was fulfilled in Isaiah's immediate future. The birth of the child is not a part of the prediction, but a *sign* that the prediction will be accomplished. Both the sign and the prophecy take place in the immediate future, that is, in Isaiah's lifetime; and there is nothing in the context suggesting the distant future or a messiah.

*Fifth*, we see that Matthew took Isaiah's words out of context. Theologians distort this prophecy as well. Isaiah's prediction is not about a birth, but about the disaster awaiting the enemies of Ahaz. The young woman giving birth is only a sign of this prediction, and the prophecy was *already fulfilled* in the lifetimes of Isaiah and Ahaz.

*In conclusion*, Matthew misread Isaiah, and the Septuagint's use of the word "virgin" is irrelevant in judging Matthew's story of the virgin birth. From the way Matthew uses other Old Testament quotations, he appears to create his story to match his quotations. The virgin birth can be only a matter of faith, but not of history, nor of fulfilled prophecy.

# Suggested References

## Books

Ehrman, Bart D., *Jesus, Interrupted, Revealing the Hidden Contradictions in the Bible (and Why We Don't Know About Them)*, HarperOne, New York, 2009. This contains a good historical account of the development of the New Testament and early Christianity.

Ehrman, Bart D., *Lost Scriptures, Books that Did Not Make It into the New Testament*, Oxford University Press, New York, 2003. This is a collection of the author's translations of early Christian writings. It is essential reading for all who study the first centuries of Christianity. It has introductory material for each document.

Ehrman, Bart D., *Misquoting Jesus, The Story Behind Who Changed the Bible and Why*, HarperSanFrancisco, New York, 2005. This book tells the story of the scribes. The author always gives clear explanations for his conclusions.

*Eusebius' Ecclesiastical History, Complete and Unabridged — New Updated Edition,* Translated by C.F. Cruse, Hendrickson Publishers, Peabody, Massachusetts, 2004. The version of Church history written by Eusebius provided the framework for historians for centuries. It is invaluable in giving us quotations from other works no longer extant.

*The New Complete Works of Josephus*, Translated by William Whiston, Commentary by Paul L. Maier, Kregel Publications, Grand Rapids, Michigan, 1999. Josephus was a Jewish historian who lived shortly after the time of Jesus. He avoided anything that would offend the Romans who supported him after the destruction of Jerusalem, but he recorded historical details not found elsewhere.

Jeremias, Joachim, *Jerusalem in the Time of Jesus,* Fortress Press, Philadelphia, 1975. This is the only work I know of that gives detailed and comprehensive information about first century C.E. social, economic and cultural life for the Jews. It is extremely well documented. Joachim Jeremias was a German Scripture scholar with a thorough knowledge of ancient languages.

Jeremias, Joachim, *The Lord's Prayer,* Fortress Press, Philadelphia, 1964. This is a small pamphlet of only 39 pages, but it gives a clear and thorough explanation of the Lord's Prayer as it would have been understood in the first century, as well as how it developed.

Jeremias, Joachim, *The Parables of Jesus,* Charles Scribner' Sons, New York, 1962. Jeremias analyzes the parables in their historical and biblical context. References are extensive.

Helms, Randel McCraw, *Who Wrote The Gospels?* Millennium Press, Altadena, California, not dated. The author uses internal evidence (information found in the Gospels) to ascertain the background of the evangelists and how the Gospels were written.

Pagels, Elaine, *The Gnostic Gospels,* Vintage Books, New York, 1979. Of special interest is the author's explanation of how politics played a role in forming Christian doctrine.

Pagels, Elaine, *Revelations, Visions, Prophecy, & Politics in the Book of Revelation,* Viking, New York, 2012. The work covers the book of Revelation and puts it into a clearly understood historical setting. The author's historical exposition sets the book apart from other books on Revelation.

Young, Robert, LL.D., *Analytical Concordance to the Bible*, Wm. B. Eerdmans Publishing Company, Grand Rapids, Michigan, 1972. A thorough and complete concordance is necessary for every biblical student. This work lists every word in the Bible in alphabetical order, along with the Greek or Hebrew word from which it is translated and a short part of the sentence in which it is used. The book, chapter and verse for each word are also noted. Since the original King James Bible is the source version, you may not find the word used in your own version of the Bible. Nonetheless, this book is indispensable for all except those who can read the original Hebrew and Greek books. The concordance also lists all the Hebrew and Greek biblical words.

## DVDs

*The following DVDs are published by The Great Courses (formerly known as The Teaching Company), 4840 Westfields Boulevard, Suite 500, Chantilly, VA 20151-2299.*

Ehrman, Bart D., *After the New Testament: The Writings of the Apostolic Fathers.*
Ehrman, Bart D., *From Jesus to Constantine: A History of Early Christianity.*
Ehrman, Bart D., *The History of the Bible: The Making of the New Testament Canon.*
Ehrman, Bart D., *Lost Christianities: Christian Scriptures and the Battle over Authentication.*
Ehrman, Bart D., *The New Testament.*
Hart, Kenneth W., *The Fall of the Pagans and the Origins of Medieval Christianity.*
Kester, Craig R., *The Apocalypse, Controversies and Meaning in Western History.*
Magness, Jodi, *The Holy Land Revealed.*
Rendsburg, Gary A., *The Dead Sea Scrolls.*

# Index

Abba, 89, 90, 92
Abraham, v, 4, 5, 8, 9, 13, 34, 35, 37, 60, 61, 70, 72, 75, 91, 92, 99, 120
Absolution, 85, 87
Adoption, viii, 89, 94
Adoptionism, 18
Adversus Haereses, 11
Against Heresies, 11
Antichrist, 100, 104
Antiochus, 5-7
Apocalypse, 95, 132
Apocalyptic, v, 5, 6, 12-15, 95, 97
Apocalyptic World View, v, 5
Apollinarism, 18
Apostasy, 86
Apostles, vi, 3, 11, 12, 15, 16, 20, 21, 29, 30, 34, 48, 57, 64, 73, 77, 79, 91, 95, 103, 107, 111, 121
Apostolic Fathers, 56, 132
Apostolic Teaching, vii, 18, 64, 77
Arianism, 19
Aristobulus, 8
Arius, 19, 20

Armageddon, 101, 104
Augustus Caesar, 32, 33
Babylon, 5, 101, 102
Baltimore Catechism, 2
Baptism, vii, 1, 13, 16, 19, 68-79, 83, 86, 87, 90, 94, 118, 123
Baptism of John, vii, 70, 77
Bishops, 3, 20, 28-30, 86, 110
Caesarea, 20, 23
Caiaphas, 54
Catholic Church, xi, 3, 20, 29, 79, 80, 85, 87, 99
Children of Abraham, v, 4, 60, 92
Christian Baptism, vii, 69, 73-77
Christian Belief, v, 12
Christian Bible, 2
Christian Churches, viii, 18, 20, 23, 85-87, 105
Christian Scriptures, 132
Christianity, v, 2, 10, 87, 96, 103, 105, 110, 130, 132
Constantine, 20, 87, 105, 132
Constantinople, xi

*False Questions*

Corinth, 27, 64
Corinthian, 27
Corinthians, 10, 22, 23, 27, 29, 64, 122
Council of Jerusalem, 26
Council of Nicea, 19, 20
Creed, vii, 3, 79, 80, 106, 107
Cyrus, 4, 5
Daniel, 3, 5-7, 16, 96
Darius, 5
David, vi, 8, 32, 34, 35, 37, 44, 46, 59-61, 63, 91, 127
Deacon, 30, 115, 116
Dead Sea Scrolls, xii, 119, 132
Didache, vi, 15, 29, 30
Docetism, 18
Docetists, 11
Douay Bible, 125
Ebionites, 4, 18, 26, 96
Ecclesiastical History, 115, 116, 130
Elijah, 4, 23
End Times, viii, 6, 95, 97, 104
Ennion, 53
Ephesians, 28
Ephraim, 127, 128
Epiphanius, 4, 18
Epistle of Barnabas, 56
Esau, 110
Esther, 126
Ethnic Jews, 8, 9, 60, 90
Eucharist, 29, 113
Eusebius, 20, 26, 115, 130
Exodus, 37
Ezekiel, 96, 98
Ezra, 4, 5

Faith, 29, 32, 38, 41, 68, 79, 80, 82, 84, 94, 106, 113-116, 125, 129
Fallers, 85
First Corinthians, 10, 22, 27, 64, 122
First Letter of Clement, vi, 27
First Maccabees, 5
First Peter, 74, 77
First Samuel, 37
First Thessalonians, 15, 28, 73
Forgive, 22, 23, 40, 80, 81, 83, 85-88, 91, 92, 106, 108, 109, 112
Forgiveness, vii, viii, 23, 68-71, 78-81, 83-87, 108, 109, 113
Fraternal Correction, 22
Galatians, 26, 90, 92
Galilee, v, 7, 8, 32, 34, 43, 52, 60, 75, 91, 113
Gematria, 100, 101
Genealogies, vi, 34, 35, 60
Genesis, 1-3, 37, 110, 118, 120
Gentile Christian, 96, 99, 103
Gentile Christian Church, 103
Gentile Christianity, 103
Gnostic Christians, 3
Gnosticism, 19, 29
Golan, 8
Gospels, vi, ix, 12, 13, 16, 27, 30, 32, 42, 43, 46-48, 50, 56-58, 61, 64, 68, 73, 75, 76, 78, 92, 106, 107, 113, 114, 121, 122, 124, 131
Grace, 116, 117
Hasmoneans, 7, 54
Hebrew Scriptures, 34, 107, 125
Herod, 32, 33, 36, 48, 72
Holy of Holies, 49

Holy Spirit, 1, 2, 17, 18, 61, 74-76, 80, 104, 117, 118
Hosea, 36
Idumaeans, 7, 8
Idumea, 7
Iesous, 101
Ignatius, vi, 30
Immanuel, 127, 128
Indulgences, 87
Irenaeus, 11
Isaac, 37, 110, 120
Isaiah, vi, ix, 36, 38, 40, 41, 46, 47, 96, 125-129
Israel, 2, 4, 7, 8, 14, 15, 25, 31, 38, 40, 41, 53, 54, 56, 61, 69, 71, 75, 91, 98, 100, 102-105, 128
Israelite, 101
Iturea, 8
Jacob, 35, 37, 110
James, 26, 35, 48, 64, 77, 96, 105, 106, 116, 119, 125, 132
Jeremiah, 23, 36, 96
Jerusalem, 4-8, 11, 26, 35, 36, 43, 44, 46-48, 51, 53-55, 64, 65, 69, 73, 96, 98, 100, 102-104, 113, 128, 131
Jesus, i, v, viii, xii, 1-6, 8, 10-26, 28, 30-69, 72-85, 87, 88, 90-93, 96, 97, 99-102, 104-108, 111-113, 116, 117, 121-123, 125, 130-132
Jewish Antiquities, 71
Jewish Law, 4, 58, 70
Jewish Messiah, 31, 34, 41, 77, 96, 104
Jewish View of Pagans, v, 8
Jews, vii, 1, 3-10, 15, 25, 31, 32, 34, 35, 41, 44, 45, 47-49, 52, 56-61, 63, 65, 70, 72, 73, 75, 77, 81, 90, 91, 96, 98, 100, 117, 127, 131
John Hyrcanus, 7, 8
John of Patmos, viii, 2, 11, 15, 95, 96, 104, 105
John the Baptist, v, vii, 4, 5, 12, 15, 23, 37, 69, 70, 73, 75, 105
Joseph of Arimathea, 63, 65, 66
Josephus, 71, 131
Judah, 5, 7, 37, 97, 128
Judas, 14, 58, 59, 121
Judea, 8, 52, 90
Judgment, 11, 13, 72, 73, 101, 102
King James Bible, 132
King James Version, 119, 125
Kingdom of God, 9, 12-14, 21, 55, 73, 76, 118
Lamb, 75, 97, 98, 101-105
Last Supper, 29, 59, 121, 122
Latin Vulgate, 125
Law of Moses, 30
Leitmotif, vi, 36, 37
Leontopolis, 54
Magi, 32, 33
Marcion, 19, 29
Marcionism, 19
Masoretic Text, 126, 127
Messiah, vi, 8, 12, 15-18, 23, 24, 31, 32, 34, 35, 38-41, 56, 58, 60, 61, 63, 67, 75, 77, 80, 91, 96, 99-102, 104, 129
Michael Cerularius, xi
Money Changers, vii, 49-53
Monophysitism, 18

*False Questions*

Monotheletism, 18
Moses, 30, 37, 76, 99, 123
Mount Zion, 101
Mt. Gerizim, 7, 47
Nathan, 35
Nativity, 32, 33
Nazareth, 32-34, 36, 52, 56, 63
Nazorean, 36
Nebuchadnezzar, 5
Nehemiah, 4, 5
Nero, 100
New Testament, 15, 16, 29, 56, 74, 95, 96, 104, 115-118, 120, 121, 126, 130, 132
New Testament Canon, 56, 132
Nicene Creed, 79
Nicodemus, 76
Northern Kingdom of Israel, 128
Old Testament, 2, 3, 5, 19, 36-38, 41, 78, 92, 103, 104, 117, 118, 126, 129
Orthodox, xi, 79
Overseers, vi, 27, 29, 30
Pagans, v, 8, 132
Paleography, 124
Palestine, 20
Passover, 43, 44, 47, 50, 51, 59, 121
Pastoral Epistles, vi, 28, 29, 116
Patmos, viii, 2, 10, 11, 15, 95, 96, 104, 105
Penance, viii, 70, 85-87
Pentateuch, 123
Pentecost, 77, 117
Pergamum, 10
Pharisee, 82
Pharisees, 13, 60, 70, 82, 123

Philip Hughes, xi
Phoenicia, 53
Pilate, vii, 34, 56-59, 61-63, 65, 80
Pope Leo IX, xi
Pope Pius XII, 3
Promised Land, 71, 72
Proselyte, vii, 8, 9, 69-71, 74, 77
Proselyte Baptism, vii, 69, 77
Public Penance, viii, 85
Punishment, viii, 9, 67, 86, 87, 96, 97, 102
Quirinius, 32
Qumran, 54, 69, 126, 127
Rachel, 36, 37
Rebekah, 120
Reconciliation, 23, 86, 87
Red Sea, 71
Remission of Punishment, viii, 86
Resurrection, vi, 3, 4, 12, 15, 16, 18, 25, 26, 31, 41, 45, 64, 67, 73-77, 79, 80, 100
Revelation, viii, 2, 6, 10, 15, 30, 73, 75, 95-101, 103-105, 131
Roman Empire, 54, 100, 103, 105
Romans, 26, 48, 63, 89, 92, 131
Rome, 20, 24, 26, 27, 41, 50, 54, 56-58, 61, 65, 96, 97, 100-104
Sabbath, 65
Sabellianism, 18
Sadducees, 13, 53, 54, 70
Salvation, vii, 67, 69, 75, 79, 98, 104
Samaria, 7, 113
Samaritan, 7, 37, 47, 113
Samson, 37
Samuel, 37
Sanhedrin, 8

Sarah, 120
Satan, 6, 102
Savior, 79, 80, 84
Septuagint, 125-127, 129
Seven Churches, viii, 10, 96, 97, 103
Siloam, 69
Simon Peter, 20, 57
Sin, vii, 9, 12, 14, 18, 22, 23, 67-69, 71, 72, 80-82, 86, 87, 90, 92, 116
Sinners, 23, 85, 87, 98
Solomon, 4, 35, 54
Son of David, vi, 32, 34, 35, 44, 46, 61, 63
Son of God, 17, 56
Son of Man, v, 5, 7, 13, 14, 16, 17, 23-25, 56, 59, 91, 101
Spiritual Adoption, viii, 89
Spiritual Path, i, viii, 106
Suffering Servant, vi, 39, 40
Suffering Servant Songs, 40
Synoptic, vi, 13, 45-47, 75, 121, 122
Synoptic Gospels, vi, 13, 46, 47, 75, 121, 122
Syria, 30, 32, 128
Temple Mount, 49, 50
Temple of Solomon, 4

Tetradrachma, 51, 52
Theories of Secret Teaching, vii, 58
Theory of Peasant Rebels, vii, 56
Thyatira, 10
Timothy, 28
Titus, 28
Torah, 4, 54, 70, 72, 91
Trinity, 104
Turkey, 10, 96
The Twelve, vi, 12-15, 21-26, 30, 64, 79, 85, 91, 103
Twelve Apostles, 15, 21, 79, 103
Tyre, 51
Unjust Servant, vii, 80, 108
Vespasian, 54
Virgin Mary, 80
Vorlage, 126, 127
Wise Men, 33, 56
The Word of God, 102
Yeshua, 101
Zadok, 54
Zadokites, 54
Zealot, 57
Zechariah, 37
Zeus, 5, 7

www.ingramcontent.com/pod-product-compliance
Lightning Source LLC
Chambersburg PA
CBHW052051070526
44584CB00017B/2130